So You Wanna Be a Hustler?

Who does it? Why?

How do you start?

*What do you do without question—
and avoid without exception?*

Who are the likely clients?

How lucrative are "specialties"?

What are the traits you'll need?

What about taxes? And the law?

Hustling answers these questions—
and many, many more....

Other Books by JOHN PRESTON

Fiction
Franny, the Queen of Provincetown, 1983, 1996.
Mr. Benson, 1983, 1992.
I Once Had a Master and Other Tales of Erotic Love, 1984.

"The Mission of Alex Kane."
    Volume I: *Sweet Dreams*. 1984, 1992.
    Volume II: *Golden Years*. 1984, 1992.
    Volume III: *Deadly Lies*. 1985, 1992.
    Volume IV: *Stolen Moments*. 1986, 1993.
    Volume V: *Secret Dangers*. 1986, 1993.
    Volume VI: *Lethal Secrets*. 1987, 1993.

Entertainment for a Master, 1986.
Love of a Master, 1987.
The Heir, 1988, 1992.
In Search of a Master, 1989.
The King, 1992.
Tales from the Dark Lord, 1992. (Short Stories)
The Arena, 1993.

Edited:
    Hot Living: Erotic Stories about Safer Sex, 1985.
    Flesh and the Word: An Erotic Anthology, 1992.
    Flesh and the Word 2: An Erotic Anthology, 1993.
    Flesh and the Word 3: An Erotic Anthology, 1995. (with Michael Lowenthal)

Nonfiction
Winter's Light: Reflections of A Yankee Queer, 1995. (Ed. by Michael Lowenthal)
The Big Gay Book: A Man's Survival Guide for the Nineties, 1991.

With Frederick Brandt:
Classified Affairs: The Gay Men's Guide to the Personals, 1984.

With Glenn Swann:
Safe Sex: The Ultimate Erotic Guide, 1987.

Edited:
Personal Dispatches: Writers Confront AIDS, 1989.
Hometowns: Gay Men Write About Where They Belong, 1991.
A Member of the Family: Gay Men Write About Their Families, 1992.
Sisters and Brothers: Lesbians and Gay Men Write About Their Lives Together, 1995.
Friends and Lovers: Gay Men Write About the Families They Create, 1995. (with Michael Lowenthal)

HUSTLING:

A Gentleman's Guide to the Fine Art of Homosexual Prostitution

JOHN PRESTON

BADBOY

*Hustling: A Gentleman's Guide
to the Fine Art of Homosexual Prostitution*
Copyright © 1994 by John Preston
All Rights Reserved

No part of this book may be reproduced, stored in a retrieval system, or transmitted in any form, by any means, including mechanical, electronic, photocopying, recording or otherwise, without prior written permission of the publishers.

First BADBOY Edition 1997

First Printing March 1997

ISBN 1-56333-517-4

Manufactured in the United States of America
Published by Masquerade Books, Inc.
801 Second Avenue
New York, N.Y. 10017

Writing is like prostitution.
First you do it for the love of it,
Then you do it for a few friends,
And finally you do it for money.

—Molière

Samuel Steward gave me the most helpful guides to the world of the male prostitute with his Phil Andros books. Those volumes helped me find and define my life as a gay man when I was younger and, when I grew older and finally met Steward, he was also able to provide me with vital information on how to write about this gay life.

This book is dedicated gratefully to him.

HUSTLING:
A Gentleman's Guide to the Fine Art of Homosexual Prostitution

Author's Note

PROLOGUE—17

CHAPTER 1—THE IDEA OF IT—35

CHAPTER 2—WHAT CHARACTERIZES MALE PROSTITUTION?—39
The Sex Is Man to Man • The Client Has Relational Needs Hustling Involves Social Work, a Hint of Psychiatric Nursing, and a Lot of Priesthood • Hustlers Believe in Sex

CHAPTER 3—WHO HUSTLES?—45
Hustlers Are Intelligent • Prosperous Hustlers Are Clearly Gay • Few Hustlers Rely on Sex for All Their Income

CHAPTER 4—Variations on the Theme—57
Agencies • Street Hustling • An Unexpected Venue: Welcome to Modern America • Stripping Private Showings • Working the Phone

CHAPTER 5—WHO BUYS?—71
Older Gay Men • Traveling Salesmen and Other Out-of-Town Businessmen • Married Men • Inexperienced Gay Men • Fetishists • Birthday Presents • Horny Gay Men Couples • Groups • Straight Couples

CHAPTER 6—GRAY AREAS—93
*Bar Hustling • Bodybuilding Subsidies • Social Hustling
Adopted Sons • Fucking the Boss • Sugar Daddies
Personal Trainers • Massage*

CHAPTER 7—SETTING YOURSELF UP IN BUSINESS—105
A Place • A Phone • An Ad • Creating an Ad

CHAPTER 8—ANSWERING THE PHONE—125
*Don't Be Lured into Dirty Talk• Answer Your Questions as
a Professional • Be Especially Suspicious of Long-Distance
Calls • Questions You'll Often Get Asked*

CHAPTER 9—HOW TO HANDLE A TRICK—131
The Value of Orgasm • Out Calls • Long-Distance Travel

CHAPTER 10—MONEY—145
*Checks • Credit Cards • Meals • Bargain Shoppers
Students and the Unemployed • Couples • Barter • Putting
Out for Other Hustlers • Frequency Discounts
When Your Trick Wants to Stop Paying Cash • Pimps*

CHAPTER 11—SPECIALTIES—161
*S/M • Military Discipline • Fisting • Getting Fucked
Clothing and Footwear • Escort Services • Fantasies
Getting Shaved*

CHAPTER 12—STRETCHING YOUR DOLLARS—181
Beer or Other Alcohol • Clothing • Sex Toys • Sell Your Jockstraps and Jockey Shorts • Hustling Others • Dirty Letters

CHAPTER 13—PHOTOGRAPHY—185
Studios • Magazines • Independent Photographers

CHAPTER 14—SOME REALITIES—193
The Law • Taxes • Telling People What You Do

CHAPTER 15—WHY YOU SHOULDN'T DO IT—197
Money • False Relationships • How Do You Explain Your Time? • It's Boring • Your Lover's Going to Hate It • You Might Get Arrested and You Might Go to Jail

acknowledgments

Victoria McCarty began the process that lead to this project and has never relented in her belief that this is was a book that should be published. John Rowberry, who used to be the editor of *Drummer* when it was a decent magazine and later *Inches* and *Honcho Overload*, has been a great help in getting the book done, just because of his insistent phone calls asking when he could publish excerpts.

Tom Hagerty and Michael Lowenthal continue in their roles as constant companions. They are unsurpassed in their ability to take on the role of nudges who insist that things get done.

Richard Kasak continues to be a vehicle for free expression in this country and in my life. He makes it possible for those things which I consider important to be published honorably. If there were not a press as free as his that is willing to get my work to my readers, I doubt I would continue to have the incentive to create the work that I do. Patrick Carr and Jennifer Reut, the real laborers of Masquerade Books, have always striven to make publishing there as easy and as enjoyable as possible. I also appreciate their efforts, their kindness, and their support.

—John Preston

author's note

Hustling is a social phenomenon that has existed since the first time money, power, and sex between men were joined together—a very long time. While, at one level, this book is a series of anecdotes and good-natured advice, it's also the raw material of the future's vision of a part of our social history. I certainly mean to entertain you in this book, but I also have gone to great lengths to verify that the information in this volume is accurate. I want to make sure that a wide range of gay male sexual experience is captured for posterity.

To update the information on how to go about being a male prostitute and make sure that my earlier experiences fit in with current practice, I spoke to or corresponded with hundreds of men who have been—or still are— hustlers. Notes from these conversations and the letters men were willing to send to me in response to announcements in the gay press provided a wealth of information. That raw data will be deposited, along with my other papers, in the John Hay Library of Brown University for future use by scholars.

prologue

I discovered Park Square in Boston when I was fourteen. I would take the hour-long bus trip into the Greyhound terminal from my hometown. Family and friends thought I was visiting museums or going to lectures. Actually, I was hustling.

I had been something of a prodigy as a student. My parents, unsure what to do with an exceptional child, decided that they shouldn't stifle me or my mind. That specifically meant that they shouldn't censor what I read or wrote and that I shouldn't be subject to the same rules as other kids—at least, not any that might limit my academic and intellectual potential.

One result was that I was able to read some of the most exciting literature that was available. It was the end of the 1950s and the new writing that was coming out of Paris and New York was exciting precisely because it was so sexual. After years of Eisenhower repression, the country was finally beginning to talk about sex. There were a number of literary journals that were leading the way. A favorite cousin, a brilliant student at nearby Boston College, was my guide in discovering some of this work.

One of my favorites was the magazine called *Evergreen Review*, which was published by Grove Press. One of the writers I discovered in its pages was John Rechy, the author of *The Sexual Outlaw*, chapters of which were printed in the *Review* as early as 1958. Rechy put out the first hints as to how I might go about being gay. There were young men who sold themselves in certain places, and there were men who would pay for it, he told me. The paying part wasn't nearly so exciting as the idea of doing it, and Rechy gave some specific pointers on how to find out where men met one another in any given city.

A major locus was the Greyhound bus station; in Boston, back then, it was on St. James Street in the Back Bay. That's where I went. I had a wonderful first experience with a salesman from Hartford, Connecticut. He gave me the courage to return, and he also gave me my first fee.

I was so inept that I really hadn't been doing anything right as I tried to find someone in Park Square. He probably picked me up only because he had a champagne glow, having just been to hear the Boston Pops, where he told me he had a bit more to drink than usual. He came right up to me on St. James and offered to take me to his room in the Statler (now the Park Plaza, very often the site of gay rights conferences and fund-raisers, a fact that has always amused me).

When we got to his room, he immediately started to undress. This was a business transaction to him, not a whole lot more. I was very hesitant, which soon annoyed him. I had only managed to take off my shoes and one sock when I finally told him I had never had sex before.

He thought I was trying to lead him on. I would later learn that lying about their sexual experience is a common ploy for street hustlers who use it to increase their fee. They market themselves as perpetual virgins, trying to extract a premium each time their miraculously renewed cherry is taken. Eventually I convinced my salesman that I was telling the truth. He was delighted. I didn't understand that gleam in his eye then, but now I know he was just ecstatic over the idea of plucking my adolescent purity.

He quickly got me undressed. He wasn't a dream

man, but he had a decent body. His belly was a bit large, but it was solid. He had a very substantial cock. He was particularly impressed that I was uncut and, back then, had very little body hair. He proceeded to put our bodies into position for sixty-nine. I went over the edge when we had each other's cock in our mouths. I had only dreamed that it could feel so good. He then went on to fuck me, then have me fuck him. He rimmed me; I rimmed him. We had more orgasms than I could count. I tried to leave a couple times, but he always held me back. He wasn't finished yet!

I truly hadn't been looking to do anything more than have sex, but when we finally were done and I was dressed to leave, the salesman put a twenty-dollar bill in my pocket and sighed with great pleasure as he saw me out the door. I was amazed. Twenty dollars was a lot of money for a kid in 1958.

I went back to the Greyhound terminal often and walked around the neighborhood of the terminal long enough for a man to proposition me. Those men assumed that any adolescent they found in that area must be selling it. When the sucking and fucking were done and I had showered and dressed, I would always find money tastefully tucked into one of my pockets or artfully left on the hotel room bed by a departed "friend."

The money never became the reason I would go to

Park Square. I kept on going back because it was the only way I knew to get sex. That's still true for many of the youths who hustle on the streets of major cities; they are not there for the cash, they are there because there are only a few other options for them sexually. I also spent countless weekends hitchhiking aimlessly over the back roads of New England. I would wait for a driver's hand to rest on my thigh, something that occurred so often that I knew it was a way many other young men were finding sex. Get on a road to nowhere and wait for a tarnished Prince Charming to come along and kiss you out of the slumber of repression; that was what many of us did back in the fifties.

In fact, I did so very well as a hustler in those early days in Boston that I nearly got into trouble with my ever-observant parents. I had much too much cash to be explained by my one part-time job. I had no pressing need for the money. I had no way to save it: Massachusetts didn't allow banks to open accounts for a minor. Besides, my obsession with hiding my homosexual activities from my family was much more pressing than any desire to accumulate savings.

So I devised a plan. As I was returning home from each trip into the city I would take any excess money and put it in a preaddressed stamped envelope and mail off the package. I calculate that I sent something over $2,000 in anonymous cash donations to the

Museum of Fine Arts and other charities in those years of innocence.

Park Square and I got along very well for the years before I went on to college in Chicago. There, I also matriculated into cruising my peers in gay bars. Sex was still the goal, but it didn't need the cover of money anymore.

As I got older and more comfortable with sex, my days as a whore always made a very amusing conversation piece. But when I turned thirty and discovered myself living on unemployment in San Francisco after having quit my job as editor of *The Advocate*, the idea of fucking for money became a crucial issue. Could I do it? Could I live off it? What would it be like?

Of course I could do it. I had made a full-time living at it for two years. It wasn't all that bad. In a lot of ways, it was fun.

I had a guide for this new chapter in my mercenary life. I was walking down a street in San Francisco one day when a man drove by on a motorcycle. He was in full leather, even in the afternoon sun that was so warm I'd taken off my shirt. When I smiled at him, the motorcyclist made a U-turn and drove up onto the sidewalk where I was standing. I loved the overt moves he made. Of course I'd be interested in a ride on his bike, I told him, knowing full well that we were headed back to his house and an afternoon trick.

We drove back to the Castro, the neighborhood where it turned out we both lived, and went into his house. While we were clearly seducing one another, we also went through small talk. As I recall, the house was full of stained glass. Typical of gay men in San Francisco, so many of whom were into handicrafts, it was his hobby to make the stuff. The glass helped create a homey feeling to the house, not at all like the apartments of the younger men I knew who were more interested in *au courant* styles.

This man was at least forty. He was pleasant looking, and he wore his leather well, but he also had a belly on him. I was sexually intrigued, even though we both made it obvious that we were each interested in being on top. There was a definite role conflict present. I was still interested, though, especially when he told me that there was something I might want to know about him. What? That he was a hustler.

I was dumbfounded. To me, hustling was something that attractive young men did—in fact, men who were very attractive and very young. This guy was simply too old. Except for one thing: he was a leather top. He wasn't selling his body the way a younger man would, he explained; he was putting a charge on his expertise, not his appearance. He also told me it helped that he had a playroom, a dungeon where he had the props for sex that so many men were willing to pay for.

When I assured him that I wasn't turned off by his occupation, he offered me a demonstration. Why not? I was an adventurer in a city of adventure. He led me downstairs to the basement. It was a wonderfully decorated theatrical space, dominated by a rack in the center and with rough wooden walls on which he displayed a wide range of whips and other implements.

I stripped. He stretched me out carefully on his rack. It was an ingenious device. There were chains that ran from ceiling to floor at all four corners of the flat wooden bed, which was divided into three sections. After my wrists and ankles had been attached to the chains with manacles, my friend released the ends of the platform, which folded down. I was left attached to the chains with only my midsection still held up by the stand.

The music was perfect—Gregorian chants, as I recall. (I later found out that he was a defrocked minister, which helped to explain the love of ritual and the religious music.) The man was good at what he did. Nothing was violent; pain seemed to be only a punctuation point in the full body experience he gave me—hot wax mixing with sensual massage.

When we were done, he was disappointed when I declined a repeat performance the next day. He asked if I would at least be interested in working with him. It had been fun, but I assured him I wasn't slave material. If I was so adamant about my role that I wasn't willing to have a relationship as his bottom, maybe I wanted to be his sidekick. In return, he would show me the tricks of the trade; perhaps I would want to try all this myself. I decided to continue with the adventure.

The most important thing in being a leather hustler, he explained to me, was the costuming. On the first night that he had convinced one of his regular clients to hire both of us, I showed up in jeans and boots, chaps, and vest. My mentor was wearing all the same and a particularly vicious-looking motorcycle cap.

The client had been here before, so he knew where the entrance to the dungeon was. He knocked on the door at exactly the right time. My mentor let him in. There, standing in front of the client, was his fantasy: two leather tops, in full regalia, standing in the dungeon waiting for him to perform whatever duties they demanded. The customer was shivering with excitement and anticipation. He wasn't a bad-looking man. He was a bit pale, and he had an air about him of an office worker whose greatest thrill was creating a new filing system. But I admired him. After all, he had been willing to cross the line and enter into a world of sexual outlaws. That alone, I thought, indicated that he had something interesting in him.

In fact, I was turned on by his agitation. His eyes

moved quickly over our costumed bodies and around the room with all its props. I could see how intrigued he was by the paddles and riding crops, how inspired he was becoming by the black leather hoods and restraints. The man had entered into his secret world, and it met his expectations. He was delirious to be here with us.

There was a carefully orchestrated dance that lead up to the client's being handcuffed and forced to his knees. I ended up fucking him while he sucked off the other top. When we were both done, and not before, we let him lie on the floor and lick our boots, one pair on either side of his face, while he jerked off. He was enraptured by the experience and paid our fee gladly.

For a while, I continued to work as an apprentice. I showed plenty of flair for what was possible and soon had clients asking to see me by myself. Within a month, I was set up in my own apartment, complete with leather and accouterments, a master for hire in San Francisco and later in New York.

When people discover that I, a mild-mannered WASP writer, used to hustle in California and Manhattan, their eyes light up and the lewd questions flow. I have come to realize that there are increasing numbers of men who aren't just asking for dirty stories they can enjoy vicariously: hustling has become something of a cottage industry in gay America, even in the age of AIDS—perhaps especially in an age of AIDS.

People are intrigued by the quick money, concerned about the dangers, seduced by the image. They want details. They want details because they are interested in the idea of hustling themselves.

Two other things happened to make me think more about my life as a hustler.

I was in Boston a number of years ago for a business meeting. I was dressed appropriately: suit, tie, polished shoes. I had some spare time, so I went to the Haymarket, a delightfully sleazy bar in the Combat Zone that, sadly, is no longer there. It was midafternoon, and I was looking for something to do for a while. I just wanted a relaxing drink, nothing more.

A very handsome young man came up to me. He was much younger than I, probably about twenty. He was friendly, outgoing, and clearly sexually interested. Now, there certainly are younger men who are mainly interested in older men, and I wasn't that much of an older man then. It could have been a regular pickup, or so my ego wanted to believe. But at a certain point my new friend made a coy announcement: he would certainly like to go home with me, but I had to understand that it would mean losing the income he would get from someone else, someone who would give him money. And he needed that income, he said apologetically.

Of course, it immediately became clear that I was the one from whom he wanted the cash. I was being hustled. I realized instantly that it only made sense. True, I was in my early thirties, hardly old enough to be unable to find my own tricks, but I was also dressed like a businessman and I was standing in a bar in downtown Boston which was not known for the high social caliber of its clientele. I was a mark. To this young man, I was an obvious trick. Why shouldn't he assume so?

I thought the whole thing was charming. I inquired into the fee that he would need—playing along with his game and phrasing it in more delicate terms. How much would he have earned if someone else were willing to pay him? He named a decent figure, and I accepted his proposal.

I discovered that I wanted the experience. I had been on the other side of this equation so often, I now had a chance to see what it would be like to change roles.

It actually was quite lovely. We went to the hotel room I already had. When we got there, he politely turned down my offers of room service. He was clearly a busy man and, while he was careful not to show too much desire to hurry, he wanted to be on his way.

I was faced with the immediate problem: what did I want? After all, here he was, a good-looking Irishman who was willing to give me just about anything I wanted, from the sound of it. I had negotiated untold numbers of sexual encounters with other men, but I found this situation awkward. The signals of regular tricking weren't here. In another—not monetary—situation, he and I would have already established a lot of what might happen with our banter during our cruising. But this was more straightforward. I was paying. I was going to call the shots.

I told him that I wanted to see him naked. He shrugged pleasantly and then undressed. I leaned back on the bed and watched, loving the luxury of having this show put on for me. When he was naked, he began brazenly to play with himself, complete with dirty talk that chronicled the adventures his dick had already had in the past couple of days, and the many other possibilities that it held out for me.

"No, don't bother," I said. I didn't want the whole performance. "Come to bed."

He also seemed awkward after I told him that I didn't want the verbal display. Having sex without the protection of verbal fantasies was obviously more difficult for him than playing a role would have been. He blushed, as though I had caught him in the middle of some naughty adolescent behavior, and then climbed on the mattress. We embraced, kissed, and I began to explore his bare skin. It was especially erotic to me to handle him that way—me totally dressed, him nude. It wasn't that he had a spectacular body; certainly there were men my own age who were better built, as they should have been, given the time they put into the gym. His youth carried him, though. I was just old enough to be able to appreciate the sweet touch of a younger man's body. There is a tautness to the skin that one can't really savor when it is part of one's own being. My own body was aging; not falling apart, simply maturing. Here was one that still had the spring of youth to it.

I was mesmerized by how hard his cock got and how long it stayed that way. It was a good-sized dick, one of those with a flared glans that make pornographers talk about mushroom heads. The skin on his shaft was almost shockingly white. His scrotum, though, was darker. It was a tight ball of wrinkled skin. He liked having his testicles played with, and I was happy to accommodate him by rolling them around in their soft purse.

I knew that he wasn't going to keep this muscle tone; he clearly wasn't doing anything to stay in shape. He was going to move toward fat, and in the near future, I thought. For that afternoon, though, I had paid my money, and I had access to his youth. I enjoyed it. I enjoyed it immensely.

Eventually I got undressed and we went about sex. It wasn't the most passionate I could imagine, and it wasn't the most professional that he might have delivered, but it was greatly enjoyable.

I was already concerned about safe sex and wasn't willing to fuck or be fucked. I was shocked when he made it obvious that he couldn't care less about safe sex. He was nervous about my health concerns.

I also wondered—I still think correctly—if I hadn't made him nervous by mentioning that I might write about our sex. Had I created too much performance anxiety?

After he left, I realized that hiring a hustler was a viable option for my future. I didn't feel waves crash on romantic rocks, nor did my earth move—but it had been exciting, interesting, and sexy to have employed another man for my pleasure. I became even more aware of the ads in the papers and magazines. Before, they had been reminders of my own past. Now they became options for my own future.

It was a bit later that I got a phone call from my friend Victoria McCarty, then the editor of *Penthouse Variations* and now also the editor of *Forum* magazine. She had a favor to ask. It seemed that a young man she knew had decided to try hustling. Victoria had been one of the people I had entertained with my accounts of my days as a prostitute. This young man didn't want the entertaining mythology, though, he wanted to know how to go about doing it; his interests were strictly nuts and bolts. Would I mind if she set up a conference call so he could ask his questions?

It sounded fine by me, and later that day I found

myself talking to her friend, with Victoria, as always, enjoying her role as voyeur on the line. Since he had asked for advice, that's all I gave him. I went through every part of the sexual life that I could think of, explaining the ads, the tricks, the procedures. He asked some specific questions, and I answered them all as candidly as I could. The conversation took perhaps an hour, perhaps longer.

As soon as we were done and had hung up, the phone rang again. It was Victoria. "You *must* write this!" I wasn't even thinking clearly. Write what? "Everything you just told that boy. It *has* to be written!"

I laughed at first, but then thought she might just be right. I sat down at the typewriter and began to put down on paper all that I had told Victoria's friend. That original document became the central part of this book. There were many reasons why it didn't find its way to print—a conflict with a publisher, the appearance of AIDS on the scene, which made me wary of the subject for a while, and other priorities kept me from publishing it.

In the past few years, I have written so many self-revelatory autobiographical essays and books that I began asking myself why I didn't pursue this one book on prostitution more vigorously. After all, I am now so exposed by my own writing that there is certainly no reason not to go into my experiences as a prostitute. I couldn't find a good reason not to return to this manuscript and resuscitate it with new data and new experiences. I know that other people's fascination with the topic hasn't decreased. I only have to look at the classified ads to know that there are many people out there who are working the phone and many more who are paying for it. A simple and clear-cut guide on how hustling works, what it's like, and how to do it seems to be appropriate now. If, after all, you are going to do something as important as sell your body, or buy someone else's for a period of time, then you should at least have access to expert advice on how to go about it.

A postscript: Victoria's friend did, in fact, go into the business. Later on, he sent me various notes and thank-you cards. I kept his address and a copy of his ad. I thought I should give him a final exam when I was in New York the next time. If one has sponsored apprentices, one does want to know how well they have learned their trade.

I called the number and made a date. Of course, he knew who I was. He actually offered me a free afternoon or evening, to thank me for my guidance. That wouldn't seem right, I decided. He was a professional, and I wanted to judge him on his own grounds. I insisted on paying the going rate.

I went to his house a few hours before I had to catch a plane home. I was exhausted after a long trip to the city with too many publishing lunches and too many late nights in the bars. I realized that while there had been suggestions of some very athletic sex, I really wasn't interested. I was horny, I did want to get off, but I just didn't want to do all that work.

After all, he was the hustler, I explained to him. What I wanted was him to be in his underwear and to give me the massage that he advertised in his ad. I wanted everything to be soft and slow and to take a long, long time.

He was more than willing. I stripped and sprawled on his bed. He got oil and began to rub me down. It was a finely wrought erotic experience. He was good at what he was doing; I was receptive to his skills.

I eventually turned over and exposed my hard cock. He slipped off his underpants then and knelt between my legs. He took both of our erections and rubbed them together with a healthy covering of lubricant. After all the foreplay of the languid massage, it didn't take long for both of us to come—especially not after he leaned over and began to suck on one of my nipples. When we were done, he cleaned me up. I dressed and paid him, and then went off to the airport, very relaxed and very happy. I had taught this one student well, I decided. It gave me a sense of great accomplishment.

CHAPTER 1
The Idea of It

Prostitution is an omnipresent social reality. As the cliché goes, it's the world's oldest profession. Male prostitution—homosexual prostitution by men for men—is probably just as old and proportionately as widespread as its female, heterosexual counterpart.

While these statements are true, they usually carry an unspoken untruth about them. America's hypocritical values insist that prostitution is a sleazy affair with nameless johns hiring desperate, ill-educated, or evil bodies for a moment's sexual release. Paradoxically, there is also another perception of the prostitute as a highly exotic sexual superstar.

Those are simply not valid descriptions of all

female prostitutes and even less-accurate portrayals of male whores. The male hustler is seldom called upon only to provide orgasm. It may be true when the clients are only seeking a quick blowjob from street hustlers, but even there a contact may be established that is more than one-dimensional.

The modern male hustler meets his clients through ads or discreet introductions. He doesn't stand on street corners in dangerous neighborhoods. He entertains in his own apartment or visits clients in their hotel rooms or their homes. He has more in common with our interpretation of the Japanese geisha than with the *National Enquirer*'s sensational headlines about white slavery. Expert sensuality is a part of the gay prostitute's reality, but so is an accomplished set of social skills.

Do you think that prostitution itself is bad? Here is a perspective from author and artist Gavin Geoffrey Dillard—like me, a onetime whore:

> Now, with mortgage, taxes, garden, and cats to feed, I find myself more behooved than ever to participate in the trials of money-gathering, selling my time, my passions and my sensibilities in more wearisome and much more emotion-consuming manners than ever I did as a paid tart.

Let's face it, in this exhausted ruin of an industrial society we are all conscripted to prostitute ourselves

—though seldom do we garner the satisfaction of a good buck, nor even the strokes that accompany the affirmations that one is attractive, sensual, and desired by another.

As a professional writer, I can find few justifications for the drudgery of word processing, for spreading my creative cheeks for inane corporate policies, for writing a song or an article that in my heart of hearts I know is not worthy of being written—who is the better for it?

But in a romantic tête-à-tête, even of the basest and most mercenary sort, souls are obliged to touch souls, human energies mingle, and passions, however restrained, do surface.

Besides, a hundred bucks for an hour of trolloping beats the heck out of the same wage for a grisly nine-to-five within the toxic air, Muzak and lighting of our modern high-rise whorehouses. And the rest of the day is left available for poetry, prayer and meditation....

I learned many things from hustling; one of them is that labor in any form can be exploitative and degrading, but the self-employed person can at least have some control over his dignity. I was a bank teller when I was in my twenties, and I held a number of other similar service jobs. Believe me, all of them were much more demeaning than being a hustler. The basic problem with being a male prostitute is your own and other people's perceptions of the occupation, not the reality of it. It can be difficult to overcome the internalized interpretation that only people with low self-esteem would sell themselves to a stranger. Forget it. Laugh all the way to the bank and, if your self-image is in bad shape, remember that someone else thought you were hot enough that he was willing to pay for the privilege of sucking your cock. That fact has a lot more reality to it than any New Age bullshit.

CHAPTER 2
What Characterizes Male Prostitution?

What is the reality of the trade? What are the dynamics that distinguish male homosexual prostitution from other forms of whoring? Those are the essential questions that many men have as they consider entering the field. They are appropriate queries. These men want to have some sense of what they're getting into; they want to know what the landscape of the occupation is like.

The Sex Is Man to Man
The hustler, with some exceptions involving younger street hustlers, is seldom a victim or a person being exploited. He will very often be approached to do the fucking—and everything that implies. He will be seen as possessing masculine power. Perhaps even more

important, he will be the person who possesses the secrets. He is the one who will discover his client's most closely guarded confidences and will act out the customer's most prized fantasies. That is *power*.

The Client Has Relational Needs

The largest groups of men who hire hustlers have enormous needs for intimacy. Because of age, social status, or inexperience in gay life, they are as desperate for affection or relationship or information as they are for sex. No matter how bizarre clients' actual sexual drives may be, safety and affection are two of the hustler's most valued commodities in his customers' eyes. The vast majority of hustlers are living lifestyles that are highly attractive to their clients. They are openly gay, live in ghettos, trick easily without guilt, and appear basically to enjoy their lives. There is a great deal of vicarious enjoyment of that life-style that is one of the factors that makes the hustler attractive to his clients.

The hustler not only has the body the client wants, he also provides an island of acceptance for the customer in a world that still scorns homosexuality. The male prostitute not only delivers forbidden sex, he also operates without judging the client's needs, social as well as sexual.

The customer also is probably anxious to have a safe sexual encounter. Here is another paradox:

Social commentators often label any kind of prostitution as a danger in the spread of AIDS, classifying whores as vectors of infection. In fact, because an encounter can be controlled by the customer who will assume the hustler's knowledge of safe sex, using a hustler can be one of the least risky forms of sexual behavior for many men.

Any hustler who forgets that he must provide more than a hard cock and a willing ass and mouth is not going to make a go at it for long. Nor is he ever going to be able to take full advantage of his opportunity. Sex is too available in too many forms for many clients to justify putting out endless amounts of cash just to touch a hard on. They want more, and they get it from any competent hustler.

One former hustler wrote me about the best advice he ever got from another hustler. His mentor told him, "If the money is the only reason you'd sell your body for sex, you might as well work at McDonald's. You have to *want* to have sex with these guys—it takes some time, at first, but I think you have the ability." In the openly sexual world of today's urban gay man, hustling still has a sense of mystery and eroticism about it. But no one should approach hustling as anything other than a job.

There is one large group of men that is different: they are the ones who just want to see if they can still do it, or if they could even do it once.

I discovered that one friend had sold himself only after I began working on this book and he heard me talking about it. He explained that he had once gone to New York and had ended up in a gay bar that obviously was home to many hustlers. He was a new face, and all the other customers assumed he was selling it. When he got an offer that was for more money than he ever thought could come from hustling, he decided to take it. My friend left with most of the expenses of his New York vacation paid for.

In one variation or another, that is a common scenario for many men who live contemporary gay lives. They decide they want to try it out, or else that they want to test their attractiveness on the blunt financial marketplace. If they get chosen, their egos have won.

Or else, they simply will be in a bar, and someone will offer them money, whether or not they were looking for it. Usually this situation involved a man who propositioned them, but who wasn't really the type the first man was looking for. When a few dollars were added to the equation, the balance was altered.

Hustling Involves Social Work, a Hint of Psychiatric Nursing, and a Lot of Priesthood

You are going to find yourself hearing confessions and detailed accounts of your clients' past sins, all with the expectation of forgiveness. You may very well be the only person in the world who knows a particular client's most secret sexual fantasies.

One of my own regular customers in San Francisco was a very well known industrialist. He and his wife each served on charitable boards. Their picture was often on the society pages of the *Chronicle*. He spent every day of his life fulfilling his social role as leader, of the community, the family, the business. In his real world, he gave all the orders and made all the decisions—except the one afternoon each week he would spend with me, sitting on the floor and doing whatever he was told, including sucking cock or licking boots. I saw a man that the world didn't know existed.

More often, my regular customers wanted a buddy more than they wanted a sexual partner. I was the one person whom they could talk to about any subject they chose. I was the one person in their lives who would accept them as they presented themselves.

Given this perception of prostitute as courtesan, I often had trouble understanding people who wanted to judge me and my profession. My willingness to argue the ethics of hustling diminished even more as I realized that the people making the making the judgments were themselves often employees of multinational corporations perfectly willing to rape the environment or defraud poor people.

Hustlers Believe in Sex

Underneath the contempt that some people hold about prostitution is a strong pattern of contempt for sex. Think about it. If you believe that sex is good by itself without needing the justification of romance, then why shouldn't it be purchased honorably from a man who sees himself as possessing something worthwhile?

The hustler sells an hour or so of his time, the pleasure of his body, and an impression of intimacy. So long as he and the buyer can acknowledge the worthiness of the product, the result should be a decent livelihood for the one and a memorable experience for the other.

I have been a secretary. I have been a hustler. Being a hustler is much better for your self-esteem. I know that for a fact.

CHAPTER 3
Who Hustles?

Many people who are interested in hustling think they can't fit the bill. They are usually operating under the assumptions that hustlers must be either dumb rough trade or that all male prostitutes are handsome enough to model Calvin Klein underwear.

Of course, good looks are important, but a decently attractive man under thirty-five can meet most expectations of a male prostitute. You can be even older and not necessarily attractive if you are especially good at a specialty. More about that later.

More important than beauty is attitude, especially your own comfort with your own body and with sexuality. Obviously you must be willing to undress in front of a stranger and go into intimate sex acts with a minimum of preliminaries. You will be expected to be an aggressive and enthusiastic sex partner whose appetite for lust must at least appear to be unlimited.

You cannot simply stand there, pretend you're a heterosexual, and let someone suck you off; that day has passed. Few gay men today are really looking for just a straight man's cock to suck. The successful hustler is a man who can make his client feel comfortable. The customer is looking for sex, to be sure, but he also wants you to provide a refuge from the world outside. He is going to expect you to give him decent conversation and general comfort. Either he is closeted and wants some appearance of closeness, or he's an out gay man and won't put up with the bullshit of the closet.

The most negative experience I ever had with a hustler was in Washington. There was an ad in a local gay paper that offered young marines for hire—evidently it was supposed to be some cooperative thing. (I would learn later that the line was used regularly by marines who were stationed in the area. They just passed it around to one another, using call forwarding, or else sharing apartments where the phone rang. It was an interesting thought, though it meant you could never really count on who was going to answer the phone.)

The man who answered came right over to my hotel room. He was very handsome, no more than twenty-five, and well built. But he was much too nervous. I tried to get into sex, but he was offended when I wanted to suck his nipples. He looked good, but he was as sexually inspiring as a length of timber. I think I actually would have enjoyed him more if he had been a little bit contemptuous, if he had been rough trade. He was just uncomfortable, and I didn't think I had been given value for my money.

If you are looking at yourself in the mirror to see if you are a potential hustler, begin by being realistic about yourself and the standards by which you judge yourself. Like many other gay men, you probably are too harsh on yourself. There are certainly whole criteria that are meaningless when you are trying to determine if you're attractive enough to sell yourself. You cannot be too hairy or too hairless. The colors of your hair and eyes are irrelevant. It doesn't matter whether you wear glasses. Your height isn't an issue. Both circumcised and uncircumcised cocks are fine. Don't let your own preferences overcome you so much that you forget that someone else may find you perfectly acceptable.

Put it this way: You are a 5'5" red-headed circumcised twenty-five-year-old with no body hair. Your image of masculine perfection is a six-foot-plus hairy-chested Italian with an uncut cock, so you feel inadequate. Keep your poor self-image to yourself. The reality is that your type can make it as a hustler. There are plenty of men who will find you exceedingly attractive.

There are only two absolutes about your physical reality: (1) You cannot be fat. (2) Your cock must be sufficiently large.

While there are some people out there who revel in obesity (they're called chubby chasers), they are few and far between. Maybe you could advertise for them, but I don't think there are enough to provide you with a living.

There is one phenomenon that might make a difference. In some cities, particularly San Francisco, "bears" are very popular. A bear is overweight, hairy, and usually bearded. His is supposed to be an image of an outdoorsman, someone whose masculinity isn't attached to Madison Avenue's concept of sleek attractiveness. He purposely breaks the standards of male beauty by asserting this new norm. There is even a magazine called *Bear* that you can find in most gay bookstores or on larger newsstands.

On the other hand, skinny is fine. You cannot be too slender: it will help some men fulfill their fantasies that you are very young.

Your cock needn't be the Eighth Wonder of the World—though you might get rich if it is. Your penis needs only to be adequate. Compare it realistically to your tricks. Is it at least equal to half of theirs? People can be overly self-conscious about how small their cocks are when they are flaccid, even though they are admirably endowed when erect. If you fall into this category, just learn to wink assuringly and quip, "It's a grower."

By the way, penis size is less of a concern if you are not circumcised. So many men have such a powerful fetish for uncut cocks that they'll forgive nearly anything, if you have foreskin.

Youth is very often one of the attributes that any customer is looking for, but maybe less than you imagine. There's no question that a twenty-one-year-old bodybuilder is going to be a major attraction for many men who pay for sex. Some customers will like the idea of someone just skirting legal age. Still, there are situations where an older man might be very desirable—in S&M, for one example.

You can also stretch reality a bit. Here is part of a letter that Thomas wrote me from Boston:

> When I was younger, I hustled off and on for a couple of years, more for the fun of it than anything else. Now I'm forty-three and it's my job, my work, my sole means of support—and I've never been happier or more content with how I earn my living.
>
> I quit an office job a couple of years ago after an ongoing disagreement with my boss finally drove me

to the old "fuck you" point of being. After a few months of pavement pounding and dwindling financial resources, I happened to pick up a local paper and came on the adult services section. I gambled seventy dollars I couldn't afford on my first ad, and had in excess of sixty calls the first weekend the ad was in the paper. I haven't looked back.

I advertise myself as a thirty-seven-year-old (well, forty-three just sounded too old) who gives the "best male massage." Initially, I thought even being thirty-seven would work against me, but age is definitely in my favor.

My clientele ranges in age from eighteen to seventy-eight, with most of them being in their late thirties to early fifties. All types, sizes, and colors—and seventy-five to eighty-five percent are married. Sometimes I feel like a daddy, sometimes a top, sometimes a bottom, sometimes a social worker, sometimes a psychologist. It's a curious business that fascinates me endlessly. I never know what to expect when I open my front door or go out on a hotel call.

Once you have established that you have the minimum requirements physically, you have to look at the rest of your package to see if it will sell. I know well over one hundred hustlers. They share some unexpected characteristics.

Hustlers Are Intelligent

Most hustlers are college graduates or students. (Remember, I am not talking about young men on the streets.) This follows from my contention that gay hustlers need to fulfill the media image of geisha to be successful. They are at the other end of the spectrum of sophistication from street hustlers, for whose clients roughness and lack of sophistication can be the attractions. Conversation and an illusion of being peers are two things that the vast majority of clients seek. They want all kinds of sex—often very kinky—but around it they want an illusion of gentility, and especially of safety.

After John Rechy's *City of Night* made its big splash, many other emerging gay authors began to write about what had been our hidden life. One of the best known—and the best—of the writers was Samuel Steward, a protégé of Gertrude Stein, who created the character Phil Andros, also the pen name the author originally used.

Phil was a hustler in the classic sense. He was of Greek descent, hairy chested, attractive, athletic. He was also well educated. Steward was writing about the 1960s and, in those days, the rough trade image was still very appealing. Phil often got into trouble with his clients when he would make the mistake of quoting poetry to them or in some other way letting them know about his education and literary interests.

But his is an image of another time. It wouldn't sell well today. (Except for those clients for whom innocence can be manifest in many different ways. While most customers are buying entrée into the gay world, there are many who also don't want to be reminded that they are actually paying for that admission. They like the idea of a sweet kid who is doing this just for a lark, or else as a passing phase. Constant reminders that this is an occupation will turn off this subgroup of customers.)

If anything, there is a propensity for artistic and literary types to be prostitutes. Writers and artists of all kinds seem to make up a disproportionate number of the male prostitutes in New York; students, especially in the arts, seem to dominate hustling in Boston; the number of self-styled poets who hustle in San Francisco is staggering. I have never met a hustler in Los Angeles who didn't claim he was waiting for a break in show business. Male whores in Miami always claim they are out-of-work models, just riding out a lull in the fashion-photography business.

Customers today seem to get off on the artistic. It's all part of the reflection of the free-spiritedness they like and even admire. Also, some of these vocations reflect the ethos of the particular city—students are emblematic of Boston, as are struggling artists a visible and obvious part of the fabric of New York's daily life. There is something *expected* about a student in Boston needing some extra cash, or of an artist in Manhattan being willing to do pretty much anything to survive on the mean streets, so much so that it becomes an appealing way for a man to enter into the life of the metropolis. Customers also seem to like political activism in this age of ACT UP and Queer Nation, something that would have appalled Phil Andros's clients.

Prosperous Hustlers Are Clearly Gay

I don't mean that hustlers necessarily fulfill old-fashioned gay stereotypes. But they do live in gay neighborhoods; they read gay magazines and newspapers; they go to gay bars; they exude comfort with their sexuality. Many customers desire this gay image because it is, to them, a chance to touch what they view as an exciting—but forbidden—lifestyle. They cannot "be gay" for whatever reason of their own, but they will delight in your stories about your life. Equally as many customers will be gay-identified themselves and will be turned off by anyone who isn't clearly comfortable in gay life.

Few Hustlers Rely on Sex for All Their Income

Hustling is a part-time job for most, a way to earn extra income and to lead a lifestyle that represents excitement and a little bit of being a sexual outlaw. Most hustlers who are in the life full-time are doing it to support some nonremunerative activity which, they would insist, is their real vocation.

Boomer hustled to support himself while he worked as an organizer for ACT UP. He couldn't arrange another job that would give him the flexibility that his activism demanded. He discovered another advantage to hustling: he was able to give many men safe-sex lectures on disease protection.

Ken had one of my favorite reasons for becoming a hustler. He had gone to Milwaukee to enter art school. One of the first things he did when he moved to the big city was to fall in love with opera. It became a passion for him, and he wanted to collect recordings of his favorite performances. But he couldn't afford the expensive tapes that he wanted so badly. He noticed that there were some pairings that were made at the local cruising park that didn't make very much sense—until he figured out that someone was getting money for the deed. Why not him? With some extra cash, he could build up his library of opera recordings.

Ken shifted his focus and began to make himself available to some of the older men who seemed less comfortable with the park than he and his own peers were. He is an astonishingly handsome man, a kind of solidly built Midwestern blond that personifies the fantasies of many gay men. He soon had a clientele that was happy to trade the cash he needed for music for the sake of some regular companionship.

Many part-timers use their extra income as a way to achieve a specific goal. I know men who saved money for a house, for extravagant vacations, or for a nest egg that would allow them to make large purchases which their normal salaries wouldn't allow.

CHAPTER 4
Variations on the Theme

Gay skin magazines usually portray male prostitution as a glamorous occupation filled with outlandishly pretty blond men whose customers come to them through benevolently administered call-boy agencies, invariably located on Park Avenue or in Beverly Hills. These agencies use limousines to transport their employees to and from their apartments. Bullshit.

Such operations may exist, and there certainly are true-life incidents of hustlers being treated to extravagant trips and presents, but basically hustling is hard work.

These are the main ways that gay-sex-for-pay is arranged with a modern hustler:

Agencies

All large cities and some smaller ones have agencies. They usually advertise as escort services. It is relatively easy to join such stables—their turnover rate is remarkably high and they always have openings—but there are drawbacks.

(1) *You will make less money.* Agencies will tell you that they have a set of regular customers whose calls will provide you with steady work. It's seldom true. They are trying to attract clients from the same sources of advertising a freelancer is using. There well might be a group of steady clients that will return to the same office for referrals, but not enough to justify the large cut in your fee that the agency will claim. Just what that percentage will be varies too widely from city to city and company to company to make any rule about what percentage is to be expected, but it's usually 40 percent, which has always seemed much too high to me. Nor will the agencies ever deliver on their promises about the amount of work they can provide for you. Some hustlers still like them because the hassle of answering the phone and dealing with the phonies is taken care of.

(2) *You will be more exposed to being busted.* Heterosexual prostitution is illegal everywhere in this country except for a few counties in Nevada, and homosexual prostitution is doubly so. Police are generally tolerant of the small-time entrepreneur making a buck at a

profession the cops know they can't eliminate. What does attract them is any hint of organized crime. That is precisely what an agency means to them. If they are going to crack down anywhere, this is the first place they'll go.

(3) *You will have less control over your customers.* When you work for an agency, you pretty much have to take whomever they send you to. One problem that is much more common than you might think is that you'll find yourself in embarrassing situations when a friend or acquaintance turns out to be the client. It happens all the time. Any man you know might be hiring hustlers. At least you can forestall this kind of predicament by recognizing someone's voice over the phone, if he's calling you directly.

You will also probably have to pose for nude photographs. Agencies usually keep loose-leaf binders with pictures of their men to show customers. Often the larger agencies will also print up flyers displaying the hustlers and circulate them as widely as possible. Where are they going to go? Who's going to see them? Don't be surprised when you end up in a magazine if you take off your pants in front of a camera. It's not going to do you much good to complain about not having signed a model release when your butt's spread over two pages of a nationally distributed periodical.

Being interviewed by an escort service isn't always

very pleasant. Here's the story of one man who tried it:

> Several years ago, in mid-autumn, I realized I had a problem. I'd go to a bar, drink too much, end up somewhere with someone, and realize I didn't much want sex. But usually I'd have it anyway. If I was going to drink, end up with some schmuck having borderline safe sex, I figured I might as well get paid for it.
>
> After informing select family and friends of my intentions, I joined an "escort service." I believe God's plans for me include a comparatively broad spectrum of jobs; so, with little apprehension, I became a call boy or, if you prefer because it's one word and easier to say, a whore.
>
> I forgot why I chose the agency I went to. Maybe the name itself hinted at ultimate fabulous glamour. I called their 800 number and spoke to someone who had a voice that was simultaneously faggier, wheezier, and more malevolent than anything you can imagine. I was given a time and address.
>
> My directions were wrong. I arrived by cab, slightly late. The area was a real skidmark on the yuppie and woofy (well-off older folk) playground called Northside. One large apartment building had a sign promoting it as an "arts incubator" or such. Private security guards patrolled the street, probably against the drug dealers, who were tenacious and straight out of central casting. Young men, head to

toe in pro sports logo, hanging on pay phones in liquor-store doorways, half absentmindedly flipped through rolls of cash, openly, repeatedly....

The interviewer was kind of punky, a ring through his nose, and was one of—if not the—sickliest people I've ever seen. The mirrors of his soul were so cloudy they could have been obscuring the fact that he didn't have a soul.

He talked briefly. He had gone to school in Tempe, Arizona, and said he'd put himself through college by whoring. Maybe he didn't always look like he did then. Maybe it's one of those things like you know, the pizza man is here and it's got anchovies on it, and just the thought of anchovies makes you wanna retch for a week, but it's late, it's within your grasp, not quite ice cold, maybe if you hold your nose it won't be so bad...

I expected sex to be approached obliquely, clandestinely, or some adverb. Escorting or any activity like that was never mentioned. I was going to exchange sex for checks.

As I expected, one certain measurement was requested. My verbal response of "big" wouldn't do.

I went to the bathroom where several porno mags waited. While one or two of them were good hard-core stuff you don't find often, the pressure and vague unease I felt prevented me from getting "ready for a reading."

The interviewer entered the bathroom and saw my problem. He understood. He asked if there was anything he could do to help. I smiled and said, quarter kiddingly, "You could get your roommate in here."

"Oh, you noticed him. He noticed you, too. He thinks you're cute. Hang on."

He left the bathroom and walked down the hall toward the living room, where his roommate had admitted me to the apartment. His roommate was a strapping thing with a full mohawk, black boots, black cords stretched tight over a big, muscular ass and haunches. The kind of creep your parents warned you to avoid.

The interviewer came back and shrugged. The roommate wasn't up for it. He'd have to do.

He knelt down and began sliding my pecker in and out of his mouth. I gave in. When he believed he had a representative swelling, he put it to the tape. I went back to my apartment, awaiting the call of duty.

(4) *It is just plain dangerous*. The police are often right: some agencies are part of organized crime. You can become a pawn in a power struggle. If you turn out to be a good money-maker, you might discover that the company has some muscle to make you think twice about moving on.

Street Hustling

Every city has an area where buyers and sellers know they can find one another. My old stamping ground in Park Square, Boston, where the Greyhound bus terminal used to be, is still going strong. New York's Third Avenue in the 50s is busy with financial transactions that have nothing to do with investing. But street hustling should be viewed as a desperate measure. The price for sex on the street fluctuates with the time of day and the amount of competition. With luck, you could conceivably turn a trick for $100 or more, it's true. But on another day you'll find the rate dropping to as little as $10. I've seen regular hustlers settle for a hamburger on a cold winter night. For one thing, the clients of a street hustler are more likely to be looking for the raw sex act and not for any of the amenities. They want a blowjob or a cock to suck for themselves, and they want it quick and cheap.

(1) *You will be more exposed.* If the police hate organized crime, they loathe obvious crime. Especially since most open hustling areas are in or near residential neighborhoods, complaints can bring a sudden, unexpected series of raids. How many times do you want to have your name on a police blotter?

(2) *It is dangerous.* Street hustling often means standing in nearly empty streets late at night. You're a sitting duck for a mugger. So far as anyone else is concerned, you're probably going to be considered as

much a criminal as a thief is. You can't expect protection. Your competition will be much younger here, but not necessarily less experienced. Many of these kids are tough. See what happens when one of them thinks you've stolen a trick, and you'll know what I mean.

There's still more danger. Street hustling often means doing it in a car or in an alley. If you are caught in the act by the police or by muggers, your problems are going to multiply.

I never had these problems during my excursions. There are reasons for it. I was a very young WASP kid. Since I was so shy that I seldom approached a man actively, there was never a complaint made about me to the police by offended heterosexuals. I think I must have attracted men who had some desire or need to take care of someone. (I had many, many lectures about the dangers of the life in my few years of street hustling.) Probably my greatest protection came from other hustlers. There were older drag queens who worked the square who would mother me relentlessly and well. They would never let me go with someone they thought was suspicious or who they knew to be untrustworthy. If you are very good looking, very discreet, young, and willing to put up with some higher risks, you might want to try the streets. I just don't think it's worthwhile.

An Unexpected Venue: Welcome to Modern America

My friend Dolores French, the author of *Working: My Life as a Prostitute*, has pointed out that the new red-light district of America is the shopping mall. It's her conviction that many women who are selling it are doing it in the shadow of J.C. Penney and Sears, right beside Bombay Furniture and behind Eddie Bauer.

There certainly is a lot of sexual activity in malls, and malls are a great place to meet people, since there's as much incentive and even encouragement to take up a conversation with a stranger in the mall as there is in a bar. Better discourse through capitalism is the key word here.

I certainly know many men who can cruise malls for sex. Regional shopping centers are a magnet for men from the country who are in their version of big-city looking for any kind of adventure they can find. I don't think you'll be all that successful in hustling the malls, though—primarily because they also function as a youth center. From the malls I have investigated, there are so many very young men giving it away that you are going to have a hard time charging money for it. Those potential customers who might have the gumption to approach you are probably there for the chicken. The modern-day mall is the pedophile's playground. So, unless you can pull off looking like a really young man, don't bother.

Stripping

Male strip joints are institutions in major cities. Many men find lucrative part-time work at the dance emporia, and that trend is increasing as more and more bars have boy dancers on specific nights. One correspondent of mine is typical of many hustlers in that he really didn't need the money that came from hustling, but he enjoyed the life. He ended up in the trade because he got a job at a strip joint.

My career as a hustler was a part of my personal revolution/liberation. I was raised in an atmosphere of somewhat decayed Victorian gentility. Being gay was not spoken of as a particular horror—it was simply one of the many things which one did not discuss—in line with the premier WASP value, the golden rule of the minor gentry: *never make a scene.*

Twenty-one was a very important year for me. Besides coming of age, I finished my graduate work, and my beloved father died, leaving me a vast old house in the country and little money.

I have always looked younger than my age. I was taken for sixteen or eighteen when I was in my early twenties. In fact, in my first teaching jobs, I was always being stopped in the halls by older faculty and asked to present a hall pass. (I finally just wrote myself one.) I began hanging around the gay theaters in New York for the same reasons anyone else does—I liked watching naked boys dance. I quickly discovered, however, that I was marketable. The other boys assumed, because I was young and looked even younger, and generally dressed as they did in provocatively tight jeans with strategic rips and a motorcycle jacket, that I was one of them. That was certainly true so long as I didn't mention being a property owner with a master's degree from Columbia and an on-again/off-again career as a schoolteacher.

I made friends with them, had sex with them as friends, and partied with them. Very soon I was turning tricks right along with them. I found I was a thorough exhibitionist and got turned on by public sex. One of the first jobs I got in the business was at the old Unicorn, which was on, I think, Forty-fourth or -fifth Street. I worked with another guy—who was *really* cute, by the way—doing a number in which he would suck me until just before I came and then would have me come on his chest. He would then dance among the audience and let them lick it off. It was a very hot routine—obviously pre-AIDS, though.

For obvious reasons, we couldn't do it more than once a night or I wouldn't have had anything left for the paying customers later on. Not being under the same financial pressures as most of the other boys, I could be a little choosy about my customers. I have never liked to be fucked by anyone and I only like to fuck really cute guys, *but* I could get it up for *anyone* to suck on, regardless of how old, fat, or toothless. In fact, there is something to be said for the toothless ones in that regard. I found that this selectivity really didn't cut much into business as a large number of men just wanted to sort of worship a young, sexy body and in fact preferred to just suck me off.

Working out of the Gaiety, as indeed out of any of the theaters, was quite simple. Between shows, you buttered up your mark and offered a "private show" in the back. If he wanted to do business, you took him backstage for a twenty-minute session and charged as much as the traffic would bear. There was good money for a blowjob and letting him caress you all over. Different guys used different personality gimmicks—I tended to look tough and threatening and quickly turned out to be warm and funny. It seemed to work for me, and customers found it endearing, in some way.

If a customer wanted some serious business—an overnighter or something like that—you could arrange it then and there. If it involved an appointment for another time, I usually tried to get a deposit to compensate me in case he got cold feet after thinking about it and stood me up.

At that time, most of the theaters expected to get a cut for the house. I was never clear whether this was really house policy or just the manager's way of ripping off the boys. In some cases it was a quota which you had to meet in order to keep your job.

There was always a lot of competition for jobs, and turnover was constant. You rarely worked one theater longer than two weeks and, of course, you had to let management do whatever they wanted with you, whenever they wanted.

Private Showings

Many men, especially those who are dancers in public, will be approached to put on private shows. While this can be a private strip show, perhaps including erotic dancing, it often has to do with a fairly innocent desire to have some naked men around as decoration. If you can get to know the people involved, this is one time when you don't have to keep the rule of not going with a group of men. This is how one hustler describes this kind of scene:

> One of the most enjoyable aspects of the business was when a buddy of mine and I began drumming up work as nude waiters for private parties. My buddy would tend bar a bit also. Usually the scene would be a very overdecorated apartment on the East Side of Manhattan with a dozen or so middle-aged men; often it would be a birthday party. We would start out wearing a posing strap and a formal shirt collar and black bow tie. Of course, as we handed out drinks and snacks, we'd be groped like crazy. We would play hard to get at first, to get them warmed up, but soon the

strap came off and we would do some sort of erotic dance involving having sex with each other. After that we would let ourselves be caressed and sucked as much as the guests wanted; but if they wanted more than that, it was cash-and-carry, except for a couple of occasions when the host made an all-inclusive deal in advance for a flat rate—then anyone could do anything they wanted, whenever they wanted.

Working the Phone

In the modern world, the telephone is where the action is. Working the phone involves advertising your availability and inviting anyone interested in your come-on to give you a call to make an appointment to meet. You are self-employed, with few expenses. Your income is strictly cash. Depending on your financial needs, you can limit the number of hours you work each day. The phone can be a full-time occupation, or a lark for some extra money.

There is some exposure to being busted, but it is considerably less than with any of the other options. There is much more annoyance than there would be working through an agency, but much less potential for real trouble.

Working the phone is the meat of this book.

CHAPTER 5
Who Buys?

The greatest fear of everyone who thinks about becoming a hustler is that all the customers are going to be aged trolls. That is, after all, the American concept of the prostitute's dirty old man. The overwhelming testimony of the men I've talked to follows what I experienced myself: most of the customers are between thirty and fifty years of age. Aside from age, the buyers are a diverse group. Any gay man reading the following descriptions of who buys will see why paying a hustler can make sense for many different men.

Older Gay Men

Let's get this one out of the way first. Yes, some customers are over fifty. But they are probably the least hassling of all categories. They are also the most likely to become repeaters, a habit that will be important if you are establishing a steady income base.

Like many other young men, I was worried about older men. Would I be able to respond? Would they be strange? Would I even want to touch them? I quickly learned one of the great lessons of my sexual life: every man has something about him that is attractive and sexy. *Every man*. Sometimes men—even otherwise-attractive ones—don't take care of themselves. I have discovered that the most common type of client that a hustler will turn away will be the man who is so dirty that he smells. If the potential customer can't even bathe, then others don't want anything to do with him. But, aside from that, the point still remains: you can find something attractive about almost any man who shows up at your door. You have to change your head around about it. It's an interesting reverse from the usual situation where we are trying to decide if we want to go home with someone in a bar or at a party or have sex with someone in a relationship: we usually begin with what's wrong with this man. What might make him unacceptable? In hustling, you look instead for what makes the man desirable. What is so intriguing about it all is that you will find attractive aspects of men that you probably would have overlooked in another context. You begin with trying to find a reason to have sex with someone, not with trying to judge him.

What kind of thing? I discovered that older men—men over fifty—often had unusual and unusually large balls. It must have something to do with age. Their testicles and scrotums were just fascinating. Nipples are often a part of a man's body that you can focus on. If you find a particularly perky set of tits, you can overlook a bulging belly. It's amazing how nice a man's ass can be, even if the rest of his body isn't in the best of shape. A man can smell good; the odor alone can be something worthwhile. We each have something about ourselves that is uniquely ours, and is worth someone else's time to admire. It is the hustler's job to find just what that is in each of his clients.

Most older men who pay for sex have long since worked through their guilt trips about doing so. They like easy sex, and they don't like to spend hours competing for tricks in youth-obsessed bars. They know why they have come to you, and they are happy—even appreciative—that you are available. That appreciation can be converted quickly to lucrative regular visits if the men are treated with a modicum of respect and decency. They seldom have outlandish requests and are often pleased by the simplest fetishes and a quick opportunity to suck cock. They are the group for whom conversation and the impression of friendliness is most important.

Traveling Salesmen and Other Out-of-Town Businessmen

It may sound like a cliché, but it's very real: something happens to an otherwise-bland, middle-class man when he is packed off on an expense-account trip. You can almost hear him saying to himself: "Here I am, an up-and-coming executive. This fancy hotel room is proof of my status. No one would notice an extra dinner guest on the tab. I should call a hustler and show off a bit." Also, the men often have crowded schedules that make an evening of cruising undesirable. They are seldom a problem and they are a major source of your income.

These guys can be fun. They think that it's a bit risqué of them to be hiring someone. They also like to show off their success. And they often want much more than sex. While they display a bit of bravado in their willingness to spend some money in a way they usually wouldn't, they are also often simply lonely when they're in a strange city and, actually, are more interested in having dinner with someone who can carry on a decent conversation than they are in orgasm.

They are also great clients to have because they repeat. Once they meet someone they find comfortable to be with, they don't really want to go out looking for someone else.

I had a regular client in San Francisco who was delighted when we made contact. He was a bit shy about the whole scene, though. It turned out that once he had opened the door to it by making contact with me, he wanted more. But he didn't want to take the chance of doing the hiring himself. He would have me go through the ads and pick out another hustler. My client and I would have dinner, enjoy conversation about politics and all kinds of other things, and then retire to his hotel room. The other hustler, whom I already had arranged for, would show up, and the three of us would have sex in some combination.

If the client really liked the guy and we agreed that he appeared to be trustworthy, I would leave them together, my fee in my pocket. I wouldn't have to do anything other than entertain the client over our meal and make his date for him. If the hustler was on the sleazy side, then I would often be the one to have sex with him; the client would simply jerk off while he watched us go through some basic S/M routines. Or, if the situation felt all right, we would all three get into a sex scene together.

Married Men

Married men come in all ages, sizes, and shapes. These guys have made a compromise with society which, at least in their own heads, forces them to seek gay sex with the least possible chance of being discovered. They are often honestly bisexual. Some would have been gay if gay activism had reached them a few years earlier, before they married women and fathered children to whom they feel a deep obligation and often an abiding love. For these men the issues are complex; it's not fair or realistic to dismiss them with disparaging remarks about closet cases. Save that for people who are self-deceivers or outright liars.

These married men won't go to bars where they would risk meeting someone they know. They have constructed emotional barriers to prevent any attachment that would threaten their families.

The single most poignant interaction I had as a hustler was with a guy who was married. He was one of the most handsome men I have ever slept with—about thirty, with a breathtaking body and classically attractive face. I was usually skeptical of my customers' stories, but I believed him. For one thing, his was complete with pictures and other documentation.

He came from a small Midwestern city and had a strong traditional family background. All his values pointed to marriage and children. It was a pleasant prospect for him. If only his friends hadn't look so good in the locker room. I have listened to literally hundreds of coming-out stories. This man's narrative was markedly different from most others. His homosexual desires were only a little nudge, far from a compulsion or a drive that was strong enough that it would lead him to want to come out. His heterosexual drives were far more compelling. He followed the more powerful impulses and married his childhood sweetheart.

Then, on his honeymoon in San Francisco, he discovered hustlers when he picked up one of the many sex newspapers that are distributed for free in sidewalk racks in San Francisco and other cities. It solved his one slight problem. He had no trouble convincing his wife that a trip to the Bay Area should become part of their annual vacation. On each trip, he would claim a single day for himself. He hired me for twenty-four hours each of the three summers I was working in California. Every year I received a Christmas card—never with a return address—and a postcard in the summer to give me ten days' notice of his arrival in the city. He swore that those annual encounters were his only gay affairs. They gave him the opportunity to have homosexual sex just often enough that he was never tempted to use the other, less-safe, less-rewarding encounters in tearooms or parks that many married men choose.

My annual visitor was totally unused to the slang and the extreme forms of homosexual activity that had become commonplace in San Francisco. I had to learn that about him from the start. My ad that he had read had offered S/M activities, including water sports—an indication of my willingness to piss on people who wanted that. When he called, that's what he read back, and he made some comment about wanting to really get into it. When people say that, they often are also including enemas in the category of water sports. I agreed.

He showed up—so handsome, such a nice hairy chest and firm buns—and restated his desires. I went about hooking up an enema bag, all the time drinking beer to get myself ready to gush on him. Finally I realized that he was getting very nervous. This wasn't what he wanted at all! What had he meant? I asked. Oh, he explained, he thought I had meant we could take a bath together. I was happy to draw back on the fireworks of Folsom Street sex and give the guy a good massage and a chance to roll around in the water with me.

A hustler's trysts with married men are seldom so romantic. Daytime meetings are frequently their favorites. They are often extremely hurried and are interested mainly in simply relieving the pressure they're feeling. Many correctly assume that the discovery of their proclivities would bring on problems, and their fear can be exaggerated to the point of distraction. They are seldom good lovers.

Discretion is a feature that all your customers will demand. For example, there is never a situation in which it is appropriate to speak to a client in a public place. If you see a photograph of one of your clients in the newspaper, it is never appropriate to tell him that you've done so if it means that you now know his real name. This discretion must be intensified when you know that the man is married.

There is one group of married men who are unlike all the rest. These are men—often with some element of a European background—who joyfully embrace America's stereotype of a Frenchman and his mistress. These men are the most generous customers you will ever find. Not only will they pay your fee, they will quickly get into giving presents. They are often attractive. The ones I knew tended to be in their forties and seemed to feel that keeping someone on the side was a fitting reward for their success and/or a measure of their social standing.

One of my most regular clients was, in fact, a Frenchman. He was married, had a great job, and was full of happiness about his life. He was very clear that having access to a young man's body was one of the prizes he expected from his success. He lived in the East Bay area and wasn't overly concerned about running into friends or acquaintances in San Francisco, especially not in places where homosexuals hung out.

He was mine when he was in the city, he told me. We would eat in gay hangouts on Castro or on Folsom, and go to gay art shows and theater. He appeared to be a very happily gay man when we were together. He was one of the men who seemed to slip out of negotiating a specific fee for me. We would do whatever I wanted when we were together, and he encouraged me to read up on restaurants or expensive shows that I would like to go to. He would pick up the tab. I often didn't even see when he put money out in my apartment—sometimes I wasn't sure where it was—but I would always discover a very substantial fee lingering somewhere. It always seemed to me that he made it larger than was normal, just so we wouldn't have to talk about it.

Inexperienced Gay Men

Coming out still isn't all that easy. Gay life may look carefree to some observers; but, to the uninitiated, breaking into it can still seem a very difficult obstacle course. It's not just a question of politics and identity. Many men just don't know about sex. They are so uncomfortable that they can't operate in traditional cruising areas. Some will seek out hustlers to get them past their inhibitions or to introduce them into the world of gay bars or other gay social circumstances.

If they are uptight about their social situations, these men will often travel to a distant city to accomplish their goal of finally having gay sex or a specific kind of gay sex they are frightened to look for at home.

Some of these men are actually virgins. If they are, then realize that you have an obligation to them. They deserve kindness, like that which my traveling salesman from Connecticut showed me when I first entered the gay world.

I was often hired by men who were barely of legal age—and I turned away others who were too young. They are fun, they are often very attractive, and they are exhausting. They want to do everything the first time. Within a few weeks after their first encounter with you, you will often start meeting them in the bars.

Boomer, a friend of mine who used to hustle in Chicago, has a story about his own experience with a young client that is typical:

> There was this kid who was living up in Evanston with his folks—I guess he was nineteen or twenty, college age, and he was going to Russia on some exchange program.... It was a very big deal for him. Well, he had been in his parents' house for four months because he couldn't stay in the dorms for some reason, and he hadn't gotten laid, or been jacked off, in all those four months. And he was pretty close to going out of his mind, which I admit is a pretty attractive thing in a guy—that sexual desperation—because, when they blow, they blow. And so I said we ought to get together.
>
> He couldn't come down to the city—how could he account for where he'd been when his parents

asked (he was, indeed, a major closet case, but he was still fairly young)?—so I agreed to go up to Evanston and meet him close to his home, which is always a pain in the butt because you never know if the guy is going to show up. I was to meet him on some street corner—talk about clichés—and when I got there I found a tall, lanky, gawky, but kind of attractive guy standing there, looking nervous with his hands stuffed in his pockets.... He was terrified, and I'm not sure if meeting me made it worse or better. I explained to him—as I do to all my clients—that I was a very discreet person and respectful of his privacy and that, while this was basically a business transaction, it was one he was supposed to enjoy, and that he ought to just relax.

We couldn't go to his house, he explained, because his mother was home, but we could try the garage, and hopefully we wouldn't be disturbed. We went into the garage, and he had that scared lust look in his eyes, like he wanted to do everything but didn't know where to begin. Every hustler is familiar with this look. But, of course, the first move has to be his, so he fidgeted a bit and finally rushed up and hugged me. It was a brotherly kind of hug, and it conveyed the kid's gratitude that I was there, for the sex part, sure, but also for being a connection to the gay world, which apparently was frightening for him.

In no time at all, my pants were down around my ankles and he was slurping away at my dick in sort of a frantic, desperate way. I could see his cock was hard—it had poked its way out of his underwear, and snaked its way down his left thigh and was leaving a large precome stain on his pants.

I don't like this habit of leaving myself partly clothed, so I stripped—and before I knew it, the kid's on top of me yelling, "Fuck me! Fuck me!" I had a hard time believing a college-age person would be stupid enough to try and have sex without a condom, but this one was. I think people think sex is like the movies, where people get so carried away that they "can't help themselves" or whatever. I've never had sex and gotten so carried away that I forgot what I was doing, or lost my rationality.

Anyway, a Boy Scout is always prepared. In no time, I had a trusty Trojan on, and the kid's butt was all lubed up. He laid me down on the cold cement floor and sat down on my cock. He was about halfway down when his sphincter muscle tightened. Sure enough, he hadn't been fucked in a while—and I thought, "What the hell!" and grabbed his thighs, forcing him down the rest of the way. Rough, I admit, but it loosened him up and the look on his face was priceless.

It didn't take him long for the first orgasm—the kid must've shot six feet in the air and I was drenched. As was the side of his mother's car. But he kept riding me, and he kept laughing, and laughing, and shooting. It was probably the longest continuous orgasm I've ever seen, and it was a major turn-on.

Fetishists

Fetishists are a big group. Essentially, they are men who have some one thing they desire sexually; but they can't get it, usually because they feel guilty about it and won't ask a traditional sex partner to indulge them. One man who used to hire me was typical. He was a well-known member of San Francisco's gay community. He had a lover with whom he had lived happily for years. He also had one secret: he liked to be pissed on. He felt so terrible about this desire that he would never mention it to his lover. It was not something he wanted to experiment with in his relationship. But the compulsion to have someone piss on him was so great that he felt he had to do something about it. He would hire a hustler. It was very simple. He would come in, we would chat, he would undress, and then he would climb into the bathtub. I would have been warned that he was coming, so I would have drunk a lot of beer or soda. That was it.

Fetishes can seem to be banal to some people—making out with someone wearing a specific kind of underwear is often big—or bizarre. You mustn't think that way. You have to think of a fetish as a need your client has, and one you are there to fulfill.

This area is so important that I have listed some of the most common types of fetish in the specialty chapter.

Birthday Presents

That's right, birthday presents. (Other similar occasions will produce this kind of present giving, especially housewarmings and Christmas.) A small but surprising amount of your business will come from being a present paid for by a friend or by the celebrating party boy himself. This category is also the one that will produce the most attractive tricks of all. They will be young and, if their friends think they will get off on this kind of gesture, they will often be good guys and uninhibited sex partners.

Like any other situation involving more than one person, there can be problems. Here's a story that Boomer tells:

> Two guys called me last spring—the one wanted to rent me for the other as a birthday present—and I wasn't sure if they were both going to bed me or what. These situations are ripe with opportunities for miscommunication. They both showed up at my apartment, and the birthday boy turned out to be a very handsome, muscular Asian man while his friend was a sort of long-haired artist white boy.
>
> There was quite a bit of awkwardness. They didn't know what to do and I wasn't sure who I was supposed to have sex with, so I asked if the gift giver was going to participate. He was shocked, almost offended, and said, "Of course not!" I shrugged—I might be a whore, but I'm not a whore with attitude. Besides, I wanted the Asian boy to myself, and I could certainly put art boy in his place.
>
> Art boy sat in my roommate's rocking chair while I let his friend undress me. It was a very strange vibe—I think they expected me to be embarrassed to be

naked. I wondered why art boy wanted to watch this. Sure enough, he got up to leave the room. But I stopped him—I said whoever pays me has to stay in the room. Ha! So he sat down and I threw a mattress down in front of his chair and proceeded to fuck the living bejesus out of his pal, making as much noise as I possibly could. You couldn't have found a better show on Broadway.

The birthday boy was fabulous, a great fuck, and most appreciative of my performance. I got off on being an exhibitionist for his little pal—for whom I hope I began a long lifetime of voyeuristic fantasies.

The ones who buy the present for themselves can be some of the most memorable tricks of your life. Once I answered the door to greet someone. The client was one of the most famous porn stars in the country. As soon as he came in and relaxed a little bit, I had to ask him why he was doing this—certainly he could have found the tricks he wanted in many places where he didn't have to pay for them. He explained that paying a hustler was possibly the only sexual experience that had evaded him in his gay life, and he had simply decided to fill the gap on his twenty-seventh birthday.

The very idea of actually paying for it will often excite men who won't even need the justification of an occasion to experiment the one time.

There was a man who I knew who was one of the stars of the bars of San Francisco. He was one of those men you see out all the time whom you know everyone wants. He was very tall and well built, with particularly wide shoulders. He had a thick mustache, thinning hair, and a delectable butt. For some reason—it's not important now—when we were talking in the bar, I mentioned to him that I was hustling. He looked at me with an overtly intrigued expression. He asked me what name I advertised under. I told him, and he joked that he might look me up.

The next day he did call. I thought he was teasing when he said he wanted to hire me—this was a man I would have given it to for free without question —but he was insistent. He came right over. I fucked him silly and was delighted to do it. When we were done, I asked him why he had been so interested and what had made him decide to hire me.

He was very forthright: If he hired me, he knew he could for once end the silly games of the bar. I might have viewed him as a star, but he felt as if he was trapped in a series of social pirouettes that he couldn't break out of. He wouldn't have to go through all the courtship and the negotiation that came with bar life. I was attractive enough to excite him, and he could afford it. And more: if he paid for it, he could decide what we were going to do. He was a very big man, as I've said, and he filled most other men's expectations of being a top. But what he really wanted was to get fucked, at least every once in a while. It was well worth the money to get his rocks off just the way he wanted to. I enjoyed his honesty when he became a regular client.

Horny Gay Men

Why should you be surprised that horny gay men would be clients? Think. It's noontime in New York. The bars are empty. You don't want to masturbate. There's a few extra bucks in your pocket and, why not? Many of the men who will show up in these conditions are guys you would find in the bars who would do perfectly well cruising for themselves at other times of the day. For whatever reason, they just don't want to go through all that hassle, or it's not convenient. They are fun, they are good sex, and they may well repeat.

In fact, these men are a lot of fun. I loved these calls. The men would often come in the morning or the early afternoon. Sometimes their desperation wasn't funny, but could reveal a problem. There is a syndrome among men who drink a great deal—the hangover hots. These are men who would have tied one on the night before and would be just desperate for sex the next day, as soon as they could get it. They would *plead* for an appointment if I even hesitated to tell them to come right over.

Other men would simply be horny. There didn't have to be a reason for it. There didn't have to be an explanation. They were just struck by the god Eros, and they had to get laid. I often got late-night calls from guys who had been on a "date" with someone who, for whatever reason, wouldn't put out. The client was driven to have sex, and for whatever reason, masturbation wouldn't do right then.

Couples

Lovers will often hire hustlers. They usually do it for a change of pace: it becomes a way to perk up their sex life. Often they will do it because they have some incompatibility in their sex life together. They will both be bottoms, and they want to get fucked. Perhaps they can fuck one another, but the act won't be convincing enough. Their answer is to hire a hustler to fuck them both—or they'll want you to be the filling for a sandwich, being fucked by one while you fuck the other.

Be aware that you are not trained or experienced in being a marriage counselor. If the couple openly understands what they want from the encounter, you could get into a fine time—lots of fun, no problems. But leave if you perceive tension between the two of them. Sometimes you will be in a situation where only one of the lovers really wanted to hire you and the other is deeply resentful. Don't let the conflict escalate in any way that could get too sticky. Get out. Leave. You are not responsible for keeping their relationship intact.

Groups

Don't get yourself into a situation where there are more than two other men in the room with you. Even if there are only two, leave the minute you feel uncomfortable. Always leave any situation where you feel uncomfortable. Your instincts are some of the best devices you have to protect yourself while you're hustling.

Here's the experience of one former hustler:

There were a number of lessons I learned. One was to avoid a certain type of man who exuded a peculiar intensity—a certain monomania, you might say. It's hard to fully describe. This type was always very banal in appearance and conversation but would seem intensely fixated on some aspect of sex. These guys were weird and made me uncomfortable. After all, one had always heard tales of monsters. Jeffrey Dahmer was far from the first. In line with that, I avoided S/M scenes, did not accept drinks or food when on the customer's premises unless I really trusted the guy. I always scoped out my escape route first thing.

Another precaution is one which I believe is quite a common saying in the field—it was told to me by a theater manager first, but I have since come across it a number of times. If you come into a room and find *two* guys waiting for you, be very careful. If you find *three* waiting, and they're smiling, get the hell out of there as fast as you can. I never had that experience, but I knew a few guys who did, in fact, walk innocently into what turned out to be heavy scenes from which they were lucky to get away. However, these occasions are rare. Of course it takes only one such occasion to work a serious mischief, so one really must be on guard.

There can be times when a group is an acceptable risk. For instance, Boomer once was hired through a trusted friend to be the boy toy for a group of Japanese businessmen who were visiting Chicago.

I went to the Four Seasons Hotel, where they were staying. I had a wonderful time. There were seven of them, all waiting for me. They hadn't wanted my friend because he wasn't as muscular as I am. They would have preferred a blond, but I have such a big dick they settled for the substitution.

I like group scenes and I have a major fetish for Asian guys. It got a good workout that night. Two of the guys were really hot, in a fuckable kind of way, but none of these fellows wanted to get fucked. It was, I guess, just a major body-worship thing. I got lots and lots of tongues licking my body which was, fabulous I have to admit. They all ended up licking my cock and balls. Having that many guys crowded around your crotch is one of the most erotic things I have ever experienced.

Straight Couples

You will have heterosexual couples approach you for sex. You decide whether you want to accommodate them. They are usually looking for someone who will have a three-way with them, usually involving the man fucking you and you fucking the woman. Sometimes they will approach you to perform oral sex on both of them.

As with gay couples, it's all a question of how much complexity you want to put up with. I found the few heterosexual couples I dealt with to be on the verge of divorce or breakup. My own experiences were so universally negative that I decided I didn't want to bother to take the chance.

CHAPTER 6
Gray Areas

There are a number of areas that should be mentioned. These are other ways that sex for pay is arranged that don't quite make it into the clear-cut categories I have described.

Bar Hustling

New York, Boston, and a few other cities have hustling bars where the exchange of money for sex is negotiated as openly as it is on the streets. (Remember, that's how I met the first man I hired myself.) Usually these bars are tacky and dangerous. They most often appear to be mob controlled. I avoid them like the plague.

Yet there are some bars in some cities that are so well established that you might want to consider this possibility. It certainly is the easiest thing if you just want to try out hustling. Many men want the experience of being paid for it, just once, in the same way that many men want the experience of paying for it. If all you are looking for is a little adventure and something you can brag about in years to come, a bar might be the best place for it. Certainly there are all kinds of bar situations where someone can discover opportunities that don't exist elsewhere.

This is the experience of one correspondent:

I was eighteen and just going to college at the University of Iowa as a freshman. I had never been away from home for very long, and I was still driving back and forth to mom and dad's on the weekends. I had never been given full rein in my life, always having someone watching over me, and for the first time I was let loose on the world. But I had a lot to learn.

I had heard about a couple of gay bars in town and decided to check them out when I turned nineteen (at the time—1983—it was the legal drinking age in Iowa) and see what the scene was all about. I later discovered that one bar had closed and the other was at the other end of town. I walked to this one, scared and nervous of something new, and went in for a

HUSTLING: A GENTLEMAN'S GUIDE...

drink. About ten minutes after I had sat down and was sipping a vodka-Coke, I was approached by an older man who introduced himself. There was small talk made until I finally noticed that he seemed a little frustrated. He then asked me to go home with him and spend the night. Not being used to this, I said no at first. He continued to let me know about all the advantages of going home with him, and I still stood on my answer. He then opened his wallet and said, "Would you go home with Ben Franklin?"

That moment was a turning point for me. I said yes and went home with the man. He was a gentle person, and this was my first time being picked up by a stranger, so it was very new and different for me. After we were finished, he gave me the $100 bill, and I walked back to the dorms where I lived.

The appeal of having sex and getting paid for it was too much for me to say no to, yet I didn't want to become a "prostitute." I did continue to go to the bar, on the same night each week, and the older man was there with his money. This happened for about two months, until he asked if he could refer me to a couple of his friends. I told him as long as they were like him, meaning nice and clean. I then had four different gentlemen paying for my services, each wanting to fill his own fantasy with me. One gave me a bath, powdered my "bottom," and rubbed baby lotion on my genitals. He then put a diaper on me and put me to bed (his bed). He cooed to me and called me his baby boy and fed me a bottle of warm milk. Another liked to take showers with me and make sure that I was extremely clean. I was usually wrinkled by the time we got out of the shower. One would take me out to eat and maybe to a movie (paying for everything), and then we would go back to his place and I would watch fuck films and he would have me blow him two or three times afterwards. For one, I just jacked off onto his stomach while he jacked off, and then I left.

One time, all four of these guys got together with me and two other guys and we had a free-for-all. It wasn't as good for me as had been the one-on-one sessions. But it was something to see three guys shoot their loads all at once.

The men I was with were straight or just coming out, so I never really had to deal with any "strange" or perverted types asking for weird things. The strangest was giving head to a guy underwater at the recreation center in the city. I always thought that I could hold my breath for a long time, and I was right! Watching someone shoot into water was fascinating.

None of this hurt my self-esteem, which was very low at the time. Having so many men tell me how good looking and hot I was gave me a sense of importance. I just regret the fact that I had been making a lot of money for having sex that I could hide from the IRS and which was more than I make now in a restaurant as a waiter.

Even less common, but apparently more attractive, are cocktail lounges, most often in upscale hotels where young men in coat and tie make themselves available to gentlemen. This is a sticky game. It depends on the benign attitude of the management, which can change suddenly. It also depends on the buyer being as aware and as sophisticated as the seller. Both parties seem to have to deal in euphemisms. There is no set fee agreed upon beforehand. The buyer must pick up cues likes: "Miami has become such an expensive place to live." (South Florida is a center for this kind of hustling, by the way, as is southern California.)

As with the more overt hustling bars, it is important that you act appropriately in such an establishment. The management can come down on you hard, and the police will not be far behind. But both kinds of bars exist—the hustler bar and the cocktail lounge/meeting place. If you have good information about your city and can find them, there is a decent possibility that you could make some regular money in one of these places. The signals are so often so subtle, though, that you really should try to find a mentor to go to one of these places with you and show you the ropes. Why not advertise for just that: ATTRACTIVE MAN WANTS HUSTLER TO SHOW HIM THE ROPES. It could work. Barter your services for the wisdom he might share with you.

Bodybuilding Subsidies

This is a southern California specialty, but I've seen it work all over the country. There is one major difference between this and other forms of hustling: the sexual contract is very seldom explicit since many of the men on either side of the transaction will insist that they are not gay. Quite simply, competitive bodybuilding is a full-time occupation with very few opportunities for the participants to make money. Gay men step in and underwrite the costs for some of the muscle men. You can usually spot the sponsors in the audience at competitions.

In return for this investment, these gay men seldom get actual sex. Apparently, they seldom ask for it. I have talked to some of the money men and asked them what they receive for their thousands of dollars. It turns out that the bodybuilders will often pose nude for their patrons. Only very occasionally will they let themselves even be touched or sucked off. The nude posings are not acknowledged as sexual treats. The rewards are most often social. The patron becomes the muscle man's "buddy." The pair spends time together; the bodybuilder will grace the buyer's swimming pool an hour a day or some such agreement. They will go to parties and bars together, where the patron can bask in reflected glory.

College and minor-league athletes can pull the same trip. So can porn stars, who will receive subtly exchanged money just for spending time with another man. You can't just decide to enter this field, you must have the body and the public stature before it is offered to you.

Social Hustling

You see it in the bars all the time. A younger and/or more attractive man with an older and/or less-attractive guy. It could be a relationship with a great deal of integrity built into it; don't let the looks of the couple deceive you. But it could also be that the younger man is spending his time with the other in return for dinner, drinks, travel, presents, or just a great deal of attention. There is never an acknowledgment between the two that this is what's going on. But it's hustling.

I know of one man whose college education was paid for by another. That education would have been difficult without the help. The donor included very few stipulations. The student had to live with him while he was in school. The younger man was free to trick with whomever he pleased, but no lover would be tolerated. I am sure that there was no sex between the two of them—just companionship, but lots of money passed hands. The student got a car after his sophomore year. Tuition and spending money were included in the deal.

Adopted Sons

When I was in college in the Midwest and having trouble with my expenses, I placed a straightforward ad in a local newspaper asking for a situation where I could work in return for room and board. I was astonished when I got three responses whose sexual intent was unmistakable. All three men offered to adopt me legally and make me their heir "if things worked out."

I never followed up on those ads. I was too young to deal with the implications, but I have indeed met pairs where this seems to be the situation. I find them to be bizarre in a strangely closeted way. Usually there is a younger man who works for and lives with an older man who has actually made a commitment to leave a business or a house in return for lifelong companionship. The relationships—I have seen only a few, and they have all lasted respectable periods of time—seem to mellow in a very pleasant way over the years. I have seen this arrangement happen only in small cities and towns far from large urban areas.

Fucking the Boss

Having to fuck the boss takes place most often in tackier gay bars and gay businesses. It's a pretty obvious situation: You want to keep working? Then you put out. In the straight world, this is called sexual harassment.

Sugar Daddies

Hustlers are often confronted with men who want to stop paying for sex with cash or agreed-upon bartered goods. It makes the buyer feel better to deliver presents instead of money. Some people skip over the cash period entirely. It's not an easy situation for a hustler to find, it's more a question of waiting for it to find you. The whole point of a sugar daddy is that he gives you so much more in noncash items than he actually would have provided you with in dollars. Trips, jewelry, and clothes are the most common. They lead up to: your own charge cards and the rent on your apartment. Most often these guys will want the facade of a romantic relationship. Just remember how hard it was when you tried to have a relationships with a man you loved, and then think what a difficult act this would be to carry off.

Do not accept this kind of relationship with a man unless it is quite clear that he can afford it. I had a couple of situations where men lived out a weird form of psychological masochism and nearly bankrupted themselves over me because they wanted to impress me with their great wealth.

Another problem with sugar daddies is that they

want you to leave hustling behind. Those married men who want the luxury of a mistress are delightful; these guys who want to take over your life and "save" you can be a pain in the ass.

Personal Trainers
Personal trainers are strictly up-to-date. One of the growing fads is for men to hire personal trainers to help them design their workouts and establish and enforce a schedule of training.

Now, if you are really a bodybuilder and if you really are willing to charge fabulous amounts of money to show someone how to handle the dumbbells, you probably are going to be hit up by some of your customers. You can certainly turn them off and be offended that they mistook the character of your services, but you might decide to earn a few tips just as easily. After all, there you are, sweating up a storm in your jockstrap and your gym clothes. Of course another gay man is going to be interested in having sex with you. This will be an especially common experience if your personal trainer ad appears in gay newspapers and magazines.

Massage
Offering in your ads to massage men is one of the easiest and least stressful ways for you and your clients to approach one another. You aren't offering

the be-all and end-all of sex; he is going to be much less concerned that you are going to be dangerous or take him too far.

Massage also works because, in fact, many clients are simply looking to be touched. *That's it.* You are not necessarily going to put yourself out there for genital sex with every man who hires you.

You must be aware of the local laws on massage and massage therapy, though. Many localities do require you to be licensed or to have training before you can offer a massage.

You should have at least elementary skills in massage if you are going to offer it to clients. You should practice on friends, maybe take a workshop that you can find advertised through your local alternative newspaper.

Never hesitate to offer a client a massage even if you haven't advertised it or mentioned it over the phone. The more nervous he is, the more appropriate it can be.

CHAPTER 7
Setting Yourself Up in Business

This is what you must have to start your trade:
A place
A phone
An ad

A Place

Discretion and privacy are two of the main assets you have to offer a customer. They are as important as your body and your looks. You can run a limited business by doing only out calls—that's the term for going to the trick's home or hotel room—but if you really want to make money, you have to provide the place. It must be an apartment. It cannot be a residential hotel room. Men who hire hustlers by phone expect some comfort, and with their concern for anonymity, they certainly aren't willing to share a communal shower.

Your place must be private. Since urban rents are often sky-high, some hustlers share apartments to cut expenses. But no trick should ever have to meet or see anyone other than the man he has hired. That is the basic rule of discretion. If you do have a roommate, you must reach some accommodation with him so he is in his room, unseen and preferably unheard by the client, or else he leaves the apartment. Never think that anyone who is buying sex is willing to have company. It does not work that way.

You must remember that the client is almost always buying your lifestyle, or his image of it. You should have reading materials that he might be interested in. You should certainly have extra copies of your local gay publication on hand. Travelers, especially, will appreciate having information on where to go, gay-owned or gay-friendly restaurants, etc. A listing of the local bars will also be important to many of these men.

You should have national publications like *The Advocate* and *Out* displayed prominently. Many of your customers will be interested in these news and feature publications. As a modern, sexually active gay man, you might not find the gay sex magazines all that exciting, but your customers most certainly will.

You should have a few copies of different titles available.

You must have safe-sex material available. You can get safe-sex brochures at your local AIDS service organization. You must take seriously the fact that you are going to be one of the most important and immediate sources of AIDS-risk-reduction information that your clients are ever going to have. They need the information. You accomplish many things by displaying it. For one thing, you announce your intention to have only safe sex. For another, you will put many men at ease, men who would be concerned that you might be risky to be with.

You should underline your commitment to safe sex by having condoms displayed conspicuously. You should have a goodly number of them. Be a sport and be prepared to give your client some extras when he leaves. It is vital that we make safe sex the norm in the gay community, and you, the hustler, as a major center of gay sex, are in a perfect place to do just that.

You should also display a number of publications that deal with sexual fetishes. In general, you want to do this to make the client feel more comfortable about asking for whatever it is that he desires secretly. You want to communicate to him that his desires are okay; they are not something that will freak you out.

If you don't think it goes with the style of your apartment to have overt sex magazines out on display, then make sure they are in your bedroom, perhaps on a bedside table. Again, one of the goals is to make your client more comfortable, but you also want to announce your availability for special kinds of sex that you find especially attractive. Put a leather publication on the table if you're open to S/M. If you are into bondage, make sure you have a copy of *Bound and Gagged* out in the open. Whatever you are willing to do, you should be able to find a book or magazine about that subject. If your client can see evidence of your interest, you are more likely to get him to admit that it's his interest as well. If it is something he feels uncomfortable with, he will be all the more appreciative and happy to have found a place where he can express himself without judgment, and he will be all the more likely to return.

You certainly should have a VCR. Just as your magazines and other periodicals will announce your own interests, or at least your willingness to indulge a spectrum of interests for your client, so will the choice of videos you have on hand. Make sure that they reflect not just your own favorites, but those things that you are willing to do for a client as well.

Your client isn't going to be all that worried about your apartment being perfect. There is, after all, the element of the exotic and bohemian that is often one of the attractions hustlers have for clients. But you should maintain at least basic levels of cleanliness.

Many men will find it charming if your jockstrap is hanging on a doorknob or over your weights. None will be upset about seeing your running clothes draped over a chair. You might even find that you're fulfilling a customer's deepest fantasies by leaving your dirty underwear on the floor of your closet. You don't have to be compulsive. But you must have a decently clean apartment.

Absolutely the least you must provide to a customer are clean sheets and clean towels. This is a must. Most hustlers underestimate how many of both they'll need when they start out. You don't have to have Ralph Lauren stuff; don't worry about doing your linen shopping at discount stores. But realize that you are going to have to change the bed very often and that you are always going to have to provide trick towels as well as bath towels when your trick wants to shower after—or before—sex. Be prepared to spend a lot of time in the laundromat, or else find a decent laundry service.

A Phone

The phone is the basic way a customer is going to have to contact you. The most important thing is that you be able to answer it, or be able to respond to a phone call quickly. Most customers are anxious to get together with you within a short time after they call.

The basic way to be available, of course, is to be by the phone in person. Nothing will make a potential customer as happy as having you answer your own phone when he calls. The most important thing is that you must never, ever use your regular phone for business. There are innumerable reasons for this. For one, you are going to have friends and potential lovers calling you—you don't want to have them tying up the line. You also want to be able to know what kind of call you are getting so you can adjust your attitude when you answer.

Most telephone companies offer special deals for second lines in the same home or office. You certainly usually have the second line unlisted for free, for one thing. (And you do want your hustling phone to be unlisted; you don't want friends and family calling information and getting your hustling number.)

Whatever you do, *never* use call waiting, that obnoxious piece of technology that interrupts telephone calls with a tone to let you know that someone else is trying to get through. You owe it to the client on the phone— and to common decency —not to be flipping back and forth between callers. You will definitely lose many tricks if you pull this gaffe.

Clients will also be very uncomfortable when they hear the clicking noises when people on the other line hang up or are trying to reach you. Until they get to know you at least a little bit, many clients will be paranoid enough to be convinced that the sounds mean you are recording their phone calls.

On the other hand, you should definitely get call forwarding if there is any chance that you might want to have your calls transferred to another number—if you want to visit a friend who is simpatico and won't mind your visit being interrupted by your business calls for instance. (But for God's sake, remember to cancel the call forwarding when you leave!)

Different cities have different variations of culture that mandate a range of other electronic communications options. For instance, in many cities—certainly Los Angeles—it's assumed that hustlers will use beepers.

Beeper service comes with many variations. The beeper company gives you a number, which your clients call. Your beeper may display the number they are calling from, which they can leave by dialing that number in to the service, or it can simply tell you to call the home base to pick up a message. You won't be bothered by jerk-off calls, and yet you will get your messages from regulars.

There are some problems. Many beeper services don't have the means to allow a caller to leave an extension number—that could be a real problem with men who are in hotels. It will do you no good to get a switchboard number when you don't know who is the actual caller. Some beepers record your caller's message and then broadcast it when you press a button on your device. Remember where you are and consider whether you do want to have the message announced in front of the other people there.

One of the best ways to handle calls is to use a voice-mail service. This way, the client gets to hear your message and can gauge the sound of your voice—often a major element in the decision about whether to hire someone. More people are getting used to voice mail; it's so often used in offices. You will also be able to check your voice-mail box often and see whether there are messages there. It's not that much better than an answering machine, but it does have advantages over some of the other options.

One of the most interesting and valuable services is the cellular phone. These gadgets are becoming more and more common, and smaller and more convenient. With one of these devices, you can answer the phone wherever you are. You can go to the beach, pass a few hours in a bar, whatever—and you won't have to worry about losing business because you're not home to pick up your calls. You are also able to give whoever is calling the impression that you are available right then and there—something that is often very important to the men who hire hustlers.

There will, of course, be times when you just don't want to talk to a client. Almost all men will respond positively to the simple statement that it is not convenient to talk at that moment. Could they call back? Could you call them later?

Watch out for one thing: most cellular-phone services charge you for incoming calls. That means you're going to be charged every time the phone rings. It would seem to make sense that you can afford this service, since more calls should mean more money, but the tolls can mount. Make sure you understand the costs and keep track of them.

The most elemental service is an answering service. You simply have a switchboard pick up your calls, and you collect your messages when it is convenient. This is not a good idea. First of all, the caller is going to assume that whoever answers the call is aware of what you're up to. He might very well begin to come on to the operator. If you aren't dealing with a gay service, that could be a problem. I have known hustlers who had their service—and the number they have advertised— canceled when their occupation has been exposed. If you are strapped for money and can use only the most basic technology, use an answering machine—never a live service.

An Ad

An advertisement is the essential way in which you have to announce your availability to your potential clients. The first thing you have to do is decide where to advertise. It's not always that simple. Different advertising vehicles will produce different kinds of clients.

Essentially, the most consistently rich place to advertise are the frequently published national publications that clients will easily find on their newsstands—*The Advocate Classifieds* and *Frontiers* are two of them. These periodicals are set up to take personals. Personal ads are often their most lucrative source of income, and they have learned to make it as easy as possible for their own customers. You can place an ad in one of them and it will probably be on the newsstand within a month or so. They are set up to accept credit-card payment by fax or 800 number.

The monthly magazines—*Mandate*, etc.—are very worthwhile, but you have to really be committed to your business to bother with them, since it will be months before your ad will appear. The national magazines have a long time between composition and publication. If you are dedicated to hustling as a career and you can afford to pay for the ads in those monthlies, then, by all means, do it.

These large gay publications will most often produce clients who are somewhat out, somewhat sophisticated, and are the least risky. The customers you attract from these ads will be just those men who you expect read them. They are the least closeted by definition, because they were willing to pick up a copy of an obviously gay magazine and take it to the counter to pay for it. These magazines are by far the most likely place to advertise for men who are traveling to your city. Men who are interested in hiring a hustler when they are away from home on business or vacation often make their plans in advance, and one of these national publications is the best way they have to do that.

Local gay publications are also often a good place to advertise. Some of them—especially *BAR* and *The Sentinel* in San Francisco—have extensive ads that attract many readers. (This is often a very important point: advertise where there are already advertisers. The presence of many hustler ads in a publication tells you that there are many hustlers who have found it worthwhile. Sometimes a hustler will decide that he is going to break new ground and advertise somewhere there are few, if any other ads. It is almost always a mistake. If there aren't ads already, it could well indicate that the publication has banned them. Or, if there are only a few ads, most likely it means that the readership isn't interested in paying for it.) Another advantage of a local publication is that your ad will appear much more quickly than in other places. You can often place an ad on Thursday that will be on the stands Saturday, if you are able to go to the paper's office. This will be vital if you ever make the mistake of missing the deadline for *Advocate*

Classifieds or any of the other national publications.

The clients you get from the local gay publications will tend to be rougher than those from the national publications. By that I mean that they are less likely to know what they want, and to be straightforward and comfortable about it. They are even more likely to be married men or closet cases. They are more likely to need to have more than a few drinks under their belt before they'll call you.

Most cities have at least one alternative publication that accepts advertising from hustlers—New York's *The Village Voice*, and *The Boston Phoenix*, are typical. Sometimes the hustler ads are merged in with ads for women prostitutes. Sometimes they are relegated to a special adult-services section. (Many gay publications segregate erotic ads in this way as well—*The Washington Blade* is one example.) These publications are sure to be the source of the most married men. This is, after all, the "safe" publication for a closet case to buy at the newsstand. He is not telling anybody anything about himself by picking up one of these publications.

Many cities—Las Vegas and Fort Lauderdale among them—also have freely circulating sex magazines. These publications are aimed overtly at the "swinging" kind of guy who likes to see big hooters and to go to strip joints. More power to them. There are often gay classifieds, including classifieds for hustlers, in these newspapers.

Hustling: A Gentleman's Guide...

The clientele you'll get from a periodical like this will be decidedly downmarket. You are most often likely to get heavily closeted men or vaguely bisexual men who are out just for a risqué experience. You should watch out for these calls—they are absolutely the ones that are most likely to produce someone who could hassle you.

(You can always distinguish the place someone saw your ad by using a different name in each one. That way you know someone calling for John saw the ad in *Advocate Classifieds;* someone asking for Jack is looking at *The Boston Phoenix;* someone looking for Jay is calling in response to a sex rag; etc.)

Many of the advertising vehicles' rules will help determine what you say in your ad. For instance, Washington, D.C., gay newspapers have severe space restrictions on hustler ads. You don't have many options when you are faced with a standard policy; your ad has to conform.

When you find consistency in the ads of a publication you are interesting in using for your ads, there's probably a good reason for it. As I pointed out, the periodical may have a two-line limit for prostitution ads. That will be obvious. Many cities and states have stringent legal restrictions on what words can be used to advertise personal services. If you consistently see a license number in an ad for a masseuse, it probably means that you must be registered with the local government in order to provide that service. Find the patterns in the ads, and you should be able to figure out the rules.

Close observation of the ads should also tell you under what heading you should advertise. Escort, Model, Masseur are all common. As I have said, they may require special consideration. Usually Escort more explicitly implies an offering of sex. You just have to study the papers that you think might work for you and figure it out.

Advocate Classifieds and *Frontiers* as well as a number of local publications have begun to accept hustler ads with photographs; often they will allow you to show yourself in the nude. This is a wonderful opportunity. By all means, use it. By all means, show off as much as you can, including your face, if you're willing. Though most of the photographs have the face cut off, those men who are willing to publish their likeness are going to be the most sought after. It's very simple: customers are worried that you are not going to really be attractive. A photograph takes away a lot of the gamble on just who you are and what you might look like. If they can *see* what you look like, they are much more likely to be interested in picking you from the numerous hustlers who are advertising.

You must have a wonderful photograph. Consult with the paper about the best way to present your

Hustling: A Gentleman's Guide...

photo. Since the reproduced pictures are very small, you should start with the smallest print you can—it will create less distortion when it's reduced. You should display your best feature. If you have a big dick, this is definitely the time to show it off—hard, if the publication will allow it. A solid stomach is a sure winner. There's nothing that communicates physical fitness better than a well-defined set of abdominal muscles. If you have a great butt, show it off. Tattoos are always a turn on; have them photographed.

Whatever you do, don't skimp on the expense of the photograph. If you use a blurred color Polaroid, if the paper will even accept such an amateurish print, you are not going to make it worth your while. This is definitely a time to seek out a physique photographer. You can probably find them advertising in the same publication.

Creating an Ad

The best way to figure out how to advertise is to look over the ads in the magazines where you think your favorite market is going to be. You'll find there are certain methods that hustlers use and you can pick up on them pretty quickly.

Here are some rules:

Begin with the basics. Your ad should mention your weight, height, color of your hair, and color of your eyes.

If you use the word "versatile," it means you're willing to get fucked. Some men just starting out think they are only indicating a willingness to go through different trips with the men they're seeing. *No.* Versatile is a code word for being willing to be the bottom.

If you are not circumcised, definitely mention it. Uncut dicks are one of the most common and most sought-after fetishes of all.

Ethnicity is often a selling point. If you are African-American or Latin, say so. If your appearance fills the expectations of a more specific ethnic or national background, it can often attract clients. Germans and Greeks are examples of favorites.

If you can carry off a specific image, use it. If you really do look like a surfer, a lifeguard, a runner, say so. Make sure you have the props to go with it, though, at least in terms of clothing.

If you went to, or even better, go to a college that will communicate a certain image in your city, name it. A Harvard boy is a certain sale in Boston; a USC athlete will never go hungry in Los Angeles.

If you mention your ass, you are inviting the client to fuck you. If you mention your own butt in any way, the client has every right to assume that you are willing to get fucked. He will have a right to think you might be willing to be fist-fucked. If you are, in fact, into your ass and you are willing to be penetrated, if that's what would make this pleasurable for you—and it is what many hustlers do prefer—then make a reference to a dildo in one way or another. If the publication won't let you do that, make sure you make it clear at the opening of the first phone call.

This is actually a kind of community service. After all, there are many men who find anal stimulation the most pleasurable activity of all, and yet the health crisis makes it dangerous. You can help out by shifting their interest to using a dildo, on yourself or on them. There's no reason for anyone to go without some kind of fun that he wants to experience, but it needs to be done safely.

Do not mention any part of your body unless it is really, really wonderful. That is, if you mention a strong stomach, you must have cut abs. If you talk about your legs or biceps, they need to be exceptionally well defined.

Any mention of a body part implies your willingness and desire to use it. If you mention your nipples or your pectorals, you are announcing that you are available for tit-play. If you mention your big feet, it means you're into foot worship and other foot fetishes.

If you talk about a big dick, make sure you have one. If you are going to brag about your cock, men are going to want to have you deliver. Mention a large penis only if you are convinced yours is much more substantial than other men's. The same for your testicles: if you say you have big balls, you had better have much bigger than average balls. If you say they hang low, they had better have a very expansive and elastic scrotal sac.

Mention safe sex. Many men who are frightened by the epidemic will seek out hustlers who begin the transaction by promising not to put them at risk. Can it still be fun? they will ask, and they will want to be convinced. I just mentioned the use of dildos as a fucking substitute, but you should also be willing and able to make condom use a high priority—something that can be desirable, not just something that needs to be done.

When I was a teenager, long before there was any hint of AIDS, more than half the men who hired me would have me wear a condom. It was *desirable* in the days when it wasn't necessary. They thought the latex covering looked wonderful on an erection. Many would love having my come trapped in the reservoir. It has always astonished me that so many men who would have sought out a hustler who wore a condom before it was a necessity, now consider it to be a burden. Help them get over it. Practice using condoms and finding ways that they can be fun and entertaining.

If you are hairy or nearly hairless, mention it. Body hair, or the lack thereof, is one of the major fetishes that many men have. Shaving your body is mentioned elsewhere, but you should mention you have a shaved torso if you do.

Don't call yourself a bodybuilder unless you really are. Some men think they can carry off calling themselves a bodybuilder just because they see the inside of a gymnasium once a week. If you advertise as a bodybuilder, the client who calls is going to have every right to know your dimensions; if you are a bodybuilder, then you should be able to rattle off the size of your biceps, waist, chest, etc.

If the phone number you advertise is an answering service or a beeper number, say so. Never expect that the client is going to understand the various electronic services you might be using. If you want him to call a number where you might not be the person answering, warn him.

Put in the hours you will accept calls. Actually, there are so many drunks and drug abusers out there that you'll still get calls at all times of the night and day. But if you put a limit on the times when you will accept calls, you can regulate at least some of them. It's also helpful for you to mention if you are only available at certain hours. For example, if you work nine-to-five and are going to be at home only after six and on weekends, say so. If a potential client calls you too often without an answer, he's going to stop calling at all. It might well be that he would have been perfect for you and you for him, if only he had known that you were there for his call.

(Many clients will not go through a beeper or a service or even leave a message on your machine. If they can't reach you themselves, they will give up.)

CHAPTER 8
Answering the Phone

One you get set up, you have to face the problem of how to answer the phone. You have the ad. You have the means to accept calls. Then what the hell do you do when the phone rings?

The very act of answering the phone often throws the new hustler into an extreme panic. He is overanxious and overly nervous. Calm down. You'll get used to it. Remember, too, that the customer is usually much more nervous than you are.

Once you do get hooked up, you are in for a very pleasant surprise. The beginning of your career is going to be your easiest time. There is a whole subculture of men who do nothing but scan the ads of major publications looking for new hustlers. They are going to be delighted to find your name and phone and will flood you with calls. (There is a special interest in this kind of thing in military towns. There is nothing these vultures love more than a marine or a sailor or another service member who is just going on the market. Some of them will even travel great lengths to San Diego and other spots for the sake of new military studs.)

But don't get your hopes up too high. These men are interested in you only for the sake of novelty. Once they have had you, they will never show up again. They do serve a good purpose, though. They are very businesslike; they have done this countless numbers of times before. They're going to be easy tricks, clear about their expectations and their desires. They will be like out-of-town tryouts for you. You aren't in front of your real audience yet: you can learn the lines with a forgiving public—and one, after all, that is particularly interested in you because you are fresh and aren't overly professional.

Keep one thing in mind at all times: after the initial rush, it may take ten phone calls to land a live trick, often many more. The phone is your selling tool. You must be polite and straightforward when someone calls, but don't overdo it. Sound friendly, but don't waste too much time trying to be seductive.

One of the most frustrating things about phone hustling is that many people will make dates and never have any intention of keeping them. God only knows all the different reasons for this, but it will happen all the time. Fewer than half the people who say they will come to your apartment will show up, the others never intended to. There are some ways you can control this:

If an appointment is requested for a time beyond three hours from the call, accept the date, but tell the potential buyer he must confirm. Don't call people liars, but if the caller's extravagant in his promises —bragging about how much extra he will pay you, for instance—discount the probability he'll show up. If the caller's request for sexual acts goes beyond what you have advertised, or if he produces any extraordinary scenario such as telling you he'll be arriving by limousine, he's probably never going to show up. (He may well drive a Cadillac, but it'll be parked blocks away from your apartment.)

Here are some more tips about phone calls:

Don't Be Lured Into Dirty Talk
If the guy on the other end of the phone wants too many details about sex acts, he's beating off. Don't go into any intimate discussions. Anyone who is answering the ad sincerely knows that you are available for sex. If the caller wants too explicit a description of your services, he's probably jerking off. The same goes for your physical description. If the caller goes

on and on about the size and shape of your cock or ass, he's not going to show up. He just wants oral satisfaction and, if you keep on talking to him, you're giving it to him for free.

Answer Your Questions as a Professional

Simple, often monosyllabic answers should be sufficient for most questions. It will reassure your most likely candidates and turn off phone freaks. Do you have a hairy ass? That's one you'll be asked often. Answer yes or no. If you go into any further descriptions of your ass, you are inviting the caller to masturbate while he is listening to you.

Be Especially Suspicious of Long-Distance Calls

The vast majority of serious inquiries are the ones who either have seen you before or want to see you within three hours or less. Men calling from far away are most often phone freaks. They will say they want to make an appointment for a week away, and they will sound legitimate, but they will seldom show up at the agreed-upon time. They are for real just often enough that you shouldn't write them off. Take the appointment, but ask for a confirmation when they arrive at the airport or hotel. You can ask where they will be staying and offer to make the call yourself, but they will seldom tell you.

Questions You'll Often Get Asked

"Will we be alone?" Assure the caller that you will be. If a roommate will be there, even if confined to his room, say so. Otherwise the trick will freak out when he discovers the deception and will think that you have set him up in some way.

"How long does a session last?" Say "an hour" or "however long it takes." Most of the time, it will be much less than an hour, in fact, though they don't want to know that ahead of time. If you are scheduling multiple tricks—one right after another—keep them an hour and a half apart, at least. You shouldn't watch the clock with the first one, but you don't want him to overlap with the next one, either.

"Do you have any drugs?" Say no, even if you do. It could be the police. Never agree to sell any drug over the phone, and realize that agreeing to provide drugs as part of your hustling is doing just that: agreeing to sell drugs.

"Do you have anything to drink?" This question is slightly sticky. He is probably asking whether you do, with an unspoken offer to bring something in particular that he wants himself. You should have at least beer, soda, and juice in your house for tricks. But, if the caller is overstating the question with special

reference to beer, he may be testing your willingness to do water sports. React according to your own desires.

"Do you have a friend who could join us?" This is a dead giveaway that he's jerking off. Tell him no. Arrange for three-ways or groups only with regular customers.

"Will you meet me in a bar so I can see what you look like?" You are a sucker if you do. This question is a trap because it sounds so reasonable. Believe me, if he does ever show up at the meeting place, he only wanted the excitement of luring you to a public place. He will give you some line about getting together some other time.

Be prepared for one other aggravation when you answer the phone. People will hang up in mid-sentence. Who knows why? Perhaps your voice didn't sound right. Maybe they finished jerking off. For whatever reason, it will happen often.

CHAPTER 9
How to Handle a Trick

Now that you have placed an ad and have had a trick call for an appointment, what do you do?

For one thing, you don't wait too long. Tricks will be remarkably punctual. There will be traffic jams and subways will stall, but if he is really late, a client will usually call to reconfirm before he rings your bell, if only from the corner pay phone.

When you answer the door you should be dressed casually—jeans, a T-shirt, and shoes or running shoes and socks will do well—unless your ad has promised something specifically different. If you pushed yourself as an athlete, you should have on a jock and some kind of athletic gear. If your ad said you were a preppie, then you'd better follow through with khakis and a Lacoste or an oxford-cloth shirt and loafers. Make sure your first impression lives up to your advance billing.

You'll find your own clothing persona as time goes on. It probably already exists—you just haven't noticed it. What makes you feel sexy is what will communicate sexiness to your customer. Wear Calvin Klein underwear, if you like that. Have on a jock, if that image makes you feel hot. Sweats are often a favorite among hustlers. They are easy to take off quickly. You can wear nothing under them, and your cock and balls jiggling under the loose covering will drive many men mad with lust; many others will be delivered to nirvana if you have a jock on underneath.

If the trick begins unbuttoning his shirt and asks where the bedroom is as soon as the door shuts, you know you're not going to have to worry about small talk, but that will be a very rare occurrence.

Once the trick is inside your apartment, you must never answer your phone. (Actually, you should unplug it or find some other way to turn it off.) He's paying for your time and attention; don't be tacky and allow yourself to be diverted. An exception: if he wants to hear you talk dirty to someone on the phone, he'll let you know. In that case, it might turn him on to hear you taking calls from other prospective clients. As in so many other ways, the customer is buying his way into your intimate life. Sex is only one of the ways you can deliver it. Listening to you handle another man just as you have handled him could be exciting to him.

Once you have a client inside, you should never answer your door. Send the person away if his knocking or buzzing is especially persistent, but never let anyone inside while the trick is still there. Never forget how important discretion is.

Take the client somewhere in your apartment other than your bedroom and let him relax. Offer him a cup of coffee, tea, or a beer. If he doesn't say anything decisive, give him as much as fifteen minutes before you suggest going to the bedroom. The impression of courtship is something most of these men want from you.

Remember that these men are looking to be shown that they are entering your private life. They do not want you to be an anonymous cock. Be prepared to give a life history. Make up stories if you want to, but never turn him off by saying, "I don't want to tell you that."

Your ad and phone conversation will have created the outlines for the sex you are going to have. With time, you will learn the various ways to discover any specific expectations, but here are some questions you must include in your opening conversation with the new trick:

"Am I what you expected?" Make sure there hasn't been a miscommunication of your image. If there has and the guy wants out, be gracious. He's not robbing you maliciously. He's either too nervous, or you are simply not his type.

"Is there anything special you want me to know?" This question gives the man a chance to tell you about a special desire. If the request is something you don't want to do, tell him so politely. If he has gotten all the way past your ad and into your living room, he's not likely to leave.

Once you go into your bedroom (accomplished by the simple statement, "Shall we?" with a smile and a nod to the doorway), always undress for the man. Stand where he can watch you strip. If you are too shy to do this, you shouldn't be in the business. When you are nude, ask him if there's something he would like you to put on. There are certain items that tricks will not consider to be very kinky, but which they will expect any hustler to have on hand to wear for them. This is a hustler's basic wardrobe:

boxer shorts
white Jockey shorts (With the massive advertising campaigns of companies like Calvin Klein, there are many more variations on this theme, and they are even more in demand. Make sure you have boxer

briefs, low-rise briefs, and the other new basics.)
jockstrap
boots of some kind
athletic T-shirt
white athletic socks
dark socks
blue jeans—preferably button-fly

There are some nonclothing items you will also be expected to have on hand:

Enema bag or some other way to douche. This is essential. Very many men will not fuck or get fucked unless the ass is clean. Many will not even let you play with their asses or be interested in playing with yours unless they knew the hole is clean. You must also demonstrate safe sex with an enema bag or any other paraphernalia that you want to use in an asshole. Make sure you explain to your client how it was cleaned and when, and with what.

Cockrings. You should have two each in metal, rubber, and leather. The customer may want it on you, or himself, or one on each of you. You can also use lengths of rawhide to create the same effect. These are great things to have around in any event. You can use them as an impromptu collar and/or leash, as a decoration, or for a number of other things. Shoe stores usually carry them, since they are often used as bootlaces, and they are often very cheap.

Dildo. Have at least one dildo of moderate size and put together a collection as you go along. As the safe-sex revolution continues, you are going to find more clients wanting to use dildos rather than fuck. It's something you should encourage. You should have as many dildos as you can afford and justify.

Titclamps. Springed clothespins will do.

Again, this is a list of items a customer will not consider kinky or outrageous. It is the essential list—far from complete, but adequate. Basically, the more sex toys you have, the better off you are.

As you get further along, your wardrobe should expand. This is the second level of basics which might not be expected, but which would be appreciated by many of the customers who won't define them as being especially exotic or as unreasonable requests of you:

torn jeans
dirty jockstrap
gym shorts
Lacoste shirt
Lycra biking shorts
specific kinds of boots—cowboy, engineer, etc.

baseball cap
mirrored sunglasses
black leather jacket
torn T-shirts
sneakers or running shoes
loafers
bikini briefs
Speedo bathing suit
hard hat
heavy black belt
running outfit

The trick's dirty talk—either verbal or body language—is going to be your best guide to what he wants and will provide you with clues to pace your sex. You'll be amazed how often he'll start to moan out his fantasy as soon as you touch him. Begin with a caress, but don't kiss unless it's very obvious he wants to. Don't hesitate to refuse a kiss if you don't want to. Strange as it seems, people who are about to go into heavy cocksucking are often not willing to touch lips.

Make sure lubricant and condoms are handy. You shouldn't have to get up and leave the room to fetch them. (But don't openly display a Crisco can unless you are willing to get into fist-fucking. Many men will take the familiar container as an invitation.)

The best way to start is to offer a rubdown. (If you have advertised yourself as a masseur, you *must* start with this.) Offer to strip down completely or to your underwear and encourage him to do the same. By the way, this is also a very effective way to calm down a nervous client. If you know nothing about massage, buy a book and practice with a friend. Any decent guide to massage will include suggestions on specific oils and other things that you can use to make the experience noteworthy. A good massage is something that many clients will appreciate enough to ensure their return.

There are a very few, very common scenarios that you will be asked to enact. The most frequent are very straightforward and probably will have been established before you began: the customer wants to suck you off, or he wants to get fucked. Your job is simply to provide him with an easy way to get from the beginning to one of those points.

You do whatever the client wants you to do so long as it isn't something that you said you wouldn't. For example, many clients don't quite believe that you won't suck them or get fucked and will make subtle moves to check you out on the acts. That will be especially true if their self-perception is such that they think they are hot enough to get you to contradict your usual rules. Just refuse the slight pressure trying to push your head down to their crotch or push away the finger testing your asshole—if you want to.

When the two of you are finished, smile. Don't

hurry him. Believe me, he will seldom have taken up his hour. Let him relax, catch his breath. When you do think it's appropriate to start him moving, do it gently by asking whether he wants to take a shower. If he doesn't move fast enough, explain that you have someone coming over soon. The threat of meeting another person is usually enough to get him to leave.

The Value of Orgasm

That's that, and you are richer and he is happier.

There is one thing that surprises most people about sex between hustlers and clients: you don't have to come. Pornography and most romantic sexual encounters place a high value on the achievement of orgasm. There will be occasional customers who will want to see you shoot; but they are a tiny minority, and they will announce that intent early on. The focus of hustling is the client's orgasm, not yours. Once he comes, your job is done. Some will be pleased if you go on, but it's not necessary; more will simply want to get up and leave, and they will want to do it so quickly that they won't even notice what you have or haven't accomplished for yourself. Since most sex acts that the client will be interested in will demand an erection on your part, you must watch yourself to make sure that you don't come well before the customer; he will be very disappointed and you could ruin everything for him if you go soft too soon.

Remember: the focus of hustling is the client's orgasm. Many men will need your assurance that you are having a good time, but if you get too much into your own trip and forget your customer's pleasure, you are going to turn him off completely—certainly so much that he won't come back a second time.

Out Calls

A lot of things change when you go to meet the trick rather than having him come to your apartment. They revolve basically around one point: he has given up his right to privacy and anonymity. If he comes to you, you should never press him about his specific occupation, residence, marital status, or last name. He will tell you what he wants you to know, and he will often lie about it. You should never ask him any of those pieces of information without his specific invitation to do so. But these rules change when you go to his place.

Those same assholes who make dates and don't show up will also call and send you scurrying off to a fake out call. If you don't take the necessary steps, you'll find yourself trying to find a nonexistent hotel room or knocking on the door of the city morgue. Besides, if you're going to his house or his hotel room, you obviously could easily discover his identity. He should realize that.

Before you leave your house, you must get a verifiable full name from the caller. Explain to the trick just why you have to check it out if he balks. Confirmation is really quite simple. If he is at a hotel, call its number and ask the hotel operator for "John Smith's room." The operator may not be willing to actually verify the room number, but he or she will put through a call to that room. You'll find out quickly and easily whether he's really there. If the client wants you at his residence, check the phone book or call information to see whether the number matches the one he gave you. In some locations, operators for the phone company will also verify an address.

There is a gray area if the phone is unlisted. Here's a hint: call information and ask for the number for John Smith at the address he's given you. The operator will usually tell you that there's no John Smith at that address before he or she will say that John Smith's number is unlisted.

You'll still get burned by pranksters every once in a while. If the call is to go very far, decline. For example, I would never go farther than a ten-dollar cab ride. Though, actually, once the trick knows you're going to check up on him, he'll usually hang up if he's faking something.

Long-Distance Travel
Of course, the great fantasy for hustlers is to be able to travel. Phone freaks know this and will play on it,

so you need to screen these calls even more carefully. Your rate for travel is three times your normal fee plus expenses for each twenty-four-hour period. Only an idiot would leave home on a long trip without a prepaid, round-trip ticket in hand.

While I was in San Francisco I had a regular trick who would fly me to Las Vegas for occasional weekends. He was a nice guy, but so shy that he wouldn't have called me at all if we hadn't been introduced by a friend of his who had hired me previously. He was a pleasant enough person with whom to spend two days. I'd get my fee, airfare, meals, a movie and a show, and a healthy tip. (Since it was Las Vegas, my tip was called "Here's some money to gamble with.") He was certainly a worthwhile and easy client.

This man asked me to come to Vegas one weekend that proved impossible for me. I knew his type, and none of the hustlers I knew personally fit the requirements. I looked through the classifieds for him to find a likely candidate for the job; he was simply too timid to do the shopping himself. I found someone and gave him a call. He put me on hold to talk it over with a friend in the background. When he came back on the line, he made these conditions: he wanted a limousine to the airport, a prepaid first-class airplane ticket, a limousine for the time he was in Las Vegas, and $1,000 a day—in advance.

If he really thought he was going to get that much,

he was wrong; but you should always be able to announce to a client and yourself just what would make a trip worthwhile. You should always be able to say that there is a cost to your time and inconvenience and, if the customer can't meet it, then you won't travel.

That is not to say that incredible trips aren't offered, but they usually happen with people who have hired you before. I was often hired by men visiting San Francisco from New York who would pay me to fly to the East Coast for a couple of days at their expense. I had my Las Vegas regular and others in Phoenix, Los Angeles, Fresno, and Sacramento. These were all clients who would rather spend more money on someone they knew and liked rather than on a less-expensive, but unknown person.

Some hustlers have much more glamorous events in their lives. When I first started hustling in San Francisco, I had a roommate who started to work his own phone after he saw how successful I was. Within a few weeks, a man he had seen no more than half a dozen times asked if my friend would be willing to accompany him on a trip. The client was an international businessman who was going on a long journey and wanted a companion.

My roommate got a two-month excursion around the world. He stayed in the best hotels and ate in the best restaurants. The trick sprang for a very large credit at Bloomingdale's for clothes ahead of time. He continually provided my friend with pocket money and gave him a four-figure tip as well. I swear it's true. (We discovered later that the trick did the same thing with a different hustler every year.)

CHAPTER 10
Money

This is the good part.

If you are working in a viable city—one large enough to support hustling—and if you stick by the phone for long periods of time per day, you will average two tricks a day per month-long period. You will go one week with three tricks a day; there will be four-day stretches without a single one. The fluctuations are a mystery. There is no rhyme or reason to it. The only thing you can be sure of is that a *very* large convention will bring business and a very sunny day with mild temperatures will cut business. Make no predictions beyond that.

The basic fact about the money every sex worker

earns is that it's cash: it disappears too quickly and too easily. The cash you can earn in a short period is going to convince you that you really don't need to stay by the phone. Give a hustler $1,000, and you get someone who is probably going to spend $1,500 without working. The illusion of endless amounts of cash is something that you must constantly battle. This is a job. You go to a job regularly. You save against a rainy day. You never let yourself and your bank account get down to zero.

You must learn right away that you can never count on being able to turn a trick every day. Never let your money get so low that you *have to* trick that afternoon. You will be having the same cash-flow problems as any other business. Also, you can never count on a particular time of day to be especially busy or slow. The minute you start making those forecasts, you will prove yourself wrong. Some people make the mistake of taking a few weeks' experience to predict their business cycles. For instance, they will assume that Sundays are worthless because there were no tricks on the first three Sundays they stayed home to answer the phone. The fourth Sunday will contradict everything they have assumed.

The one exception is the day the publication in which you're advertising hits the street. The very morning that your ad first appears, there will be a flood of calls. There is a whole group of men who do nothing but wait for new issues of the papers and magazines. In addition to these regulars, most publications will have disappeared from the stands a few days before the new issue is supposed to come out. So people will have built up their desires for a while and will be waiting for a way to buy their release.

You must come up with some kind of business plan if you're going to do this full-time. Figure out the income you need per week and take at least three tricks a day (if you can get them) until you have come up with that amount of money. Then you can answer the phone at your convenience. But until you get to that figure, answer the phone from ten in the morning till midnight with regularity.

The most important thing is to always have money for your ads. Missing a deadline for *Advocate Classifieds* or *Frontiers* can easily devastate your finances. You must always be able to pay that bill, and your phone bill. Without an ad and a phone, you have no career.

Your fee is determined by the city in which you live. Dayton probably won't provide as much as New York or San Francisco. You shouldn't hassle your fellow hustlers, but you can quickly get the range in your city by calling the ads yourself and asking each man what he charges. Don't expect them to be all that fraternal; hustlers are sometimes competitive. As much as I hate to do it, I have to advise you to lie and tell them you're a potential customer and want to know the cost of an hour with them. Ignore the rates that are published in the ads; they are seldom realistic figures. Most often hustlers who publish their rates are on the very high end of the scale and are mentioning their charges to scare away all but the most committed customers. (I doubt it's worth their while; they're probably left with an even higher rate of jerk-off calls than usual.) You will find that there is a standard rate in your city. You will gain very little by undercutting that standard. Few men are going to shop around on the phone for the cheapest whore in town; that's something they do with street hustlers. You will lose a lot of business if you go to the extreme upper figure; most men who call will know the going rate.

You need to decide how you collect your money. Many hustlers insist that you should have it in your hand before you begin to undress. If you decide that's the route you want to go, ask for your payment very politely and soften the demand by explaining that you're worried about being ripped off. I never was burned, myself, though I never made that demand. I found that many tricks like to avoid the subject of money and liked the option of being able to leave bills inconspicuously on a table or bureau. I also found that clients were more likely to tip you if money hadn't been discussed.

Checks

You must never, ever accept a check from a client. It's almost guaranteed to bounce. Especially in the age of the ATM, there's no reason why a man who claims to be able to spend good money on sex shouldn't be able to come up with the cash.

Credit Cards

You will see many ads for hustlers where they say they're willing to accept credit cards. In some cases, the hustlers have gone through the often arduous process of getting a credit-card account. They may be self-employed in some other vocation; they may have it left over from another job—something like that. Antique dealers, for example, often have credit-card accounts even when they are not expected to work at their business full-time.

You get a credit-card account through a bank. If you have a legitimate reason to have such an account, your banker will approve you. The banker will never approve you for sex work. It's an adamant stance that everyone in the credit business has taken. There is a way around this. It's called "factoring." Other people who do have a socially sanctioned business will process your credit-card slips for you. They will want a cut for their problem, a percentage from 5 to 25 percent, depending on how much they want to do it, know you, and trust you. For some reason, florists are the most common professionals involved in factoring. The essential point is that the business has to have a clientele that not only pays by credit card regularly, but also uses the phone to do so— the only way to justify the many credit-card slips that are handwritten, rather than machine printed.

If the credit-card companies find out—and American Express is especially vehement about trying to do so—you and the business doing the factoring are going to be in deep trouble. At the very least, the credit-card company will freeze the account for as long as it possibly can, just to punish both of you. It can get very sticky and be very difficult. (By the way, the most common way for a credit-card company to discover what's going on is to have a wife or parent who is responsible for the card call and complain about a charge that doesn't make sense. Often husbands or children will actually steal a credit card and then use it to buy sex, and the wife or parent will go ballistic.)

In addition to the hourly figure that is going to be your base charge, you need to establish other rates. When you are asked to take an out call, add cab fare and a bit more to achieve a round number. Sometimes a trick will say he wants more than an hour and asks for the rate for an afternoon or an evening. The rule of thumb is to charge two-and-one-half times your standard fee for a longer commitment of time. If the request is for overnight, the same fee should apply.

People who ask for these extended rates usually want a companion for dinner or lunch as well as a sex partner. Some tricks—especially out-of-towners—will want to go to bars. A few will actually just want a tour of the city. Whenever you leave your house, the clients pays for everything, and you should make that expectation very clear. If he asks for any social activity such as those I have listed, state your rate for the time period "plus expenses." He is probably already assuming this, so don't worry about it—but it never hurts to make your expectations clear.

There is one exception: If he really does want to spend the night in your apartment rather than pay for a hotel room, if it's obvious he's just being cheap about it all rather than wanting to buy the special intimacy of sleeping in the same bed with you, charge him the cost of a good hotel room on top of everything else.

With these extended rates, don't be foolish and expect your hourly rate times the actual number of hours you spend with a prolonged trick. Some hustlers will brag that they do receive it, but seldom will it be repeated. The point is that you will very seldom have a chance to turn more than two tricks in an afternoon or an evening. If you charge two-and-a-half times your hourly rate, you will almost never lose money.

Surprise! You'll be tipped the majority of times. Act grateful, but never overly so. Be gracious about it.

"Gracious" is the key word in describing how you should deal with most questions about money. Don't be greedy, but be realistic about the money you expect. It's appalling how often hustlers can be downright tacky about cash. Remember at all times that you want to secure the most dependable income you can. The best way to do that is to build up your regular clientele and not have to depend on one-timers. You build your network of repeaters by giving them a good time, showing them some element of politeness, and not trying to be too itchy about how much they shell out on each occasion.

Here are some specific money issues you will have to deal with:

Meals

For some customers, a very popular time is their lunch hour or right after they get out of work. If they especially like you, they may ask you to go out to eat with them after sex. Go if you want to; you won't overly insult them if you don't. But, for God's sake, don't expect the man to pay you for an extra hour to accompany him to dinner. The offer of a meal is a quasi-social one; it's a gracious gesture in his eyes. Of course, you do expect him to pay for the meal, and you are free to suggest an expensive one if you want.

Bargain Shoppers

You are a professional charging a fair price for a desired service. You do not negotiate that price during the phone call or at your home any more than any other professional. You have every right to expect the full fee and perhaps a tip. *Do not haggle.* Do not be intimidated by some jerk telling you you're too expensive. You already know the going rate. Stick to it. Street hustlers lower their rates on a bad day. Phone workers keep their pride.

Students and the Unemployed

You will often be asked for a special rate by students and the unemployed. If you are so inclined, this is the one time you can offer a slight discount.

I had a string of students from San Francisco State who would hire me. I had thought, the first time they called, that they were pulling my leg. But some were insistent. I learned to ask for a student ID. In some ways, that is a violation of the rules that demand that you respect confidentiality, but I learned that it wasn't as big a deal for students as for others.

The kids were great, among my very favorites. They were underage for drinking and therefore were barred from the most common socializing arenas for gay men: bars. They were also young enough that they often just didn't have the social skills to meet others and negotiate sex, even though they were young and often very attractive.

With younger men it is especially important to be very clear that this is a business arrangement. They are the most susceptible to crossing the boundaries and wanting to make what should be a financial transaction into something that they believe is an emotional commitment. Don't lead a youngster on. If the only way he feels comfortable having sex at the moment is by buying, then make sure you provide it with grace and the special care that young people deserve.

Never ever have sex with someone underage. Sex with a minor, as defined by your state's laws, is statutory rape. If it ever came to the attention of the authorities that you, a prostitute, had sex with a minor, they will throw the book at you.

Couples

Lovers will occasionally share a hustler. It's especially possible with a traveling pair. I never charged extra since my personal point of view was that the time involved was the major determination of my fee. Some people add 25 to 50 percent of their usual fees. You can make a case either way.

Couples may be great fun, but it's important for me to repeat some advice I have already given you: if you hadn't previously agreed to have sex with a couple and you find more than two men waiting for you when you arrive or when you open the door, *get out* or *get them out*. Absolutely refuse to continue if there are three or more people in a group that expects you to handle them sexually. This is a major sign of danger, an overt warning that a gay bashing may be on the way.

If someone wanted you to have sex with him and his friend or lover, he would have told you to expect that situation when he made the first appointment. No one with good intentions is going to spring this on you. If this happens, *get out* or *get them out*.

Barter

Of course barter happens. I once knew a chemist who made dynamite amyl nitrate. He would trade me four bottles for a session. Another trick owned a bookstore and would give me a credit slip in return for sex. If you would have spent the money for the goods in question, why not?

Putting Out for Other Hustlers

You'll get calls from people saying they're hustlers, too, and they're horny. They want to fuck with another pro. If they are real, they won't be offended if you check to see if they have an active ad. Do check—lots of guys will lie to you. Decide for yourself whether you're interested.

Guys who do have ads will try to get free sex by a comically obvious ruse. It's so common that I used to laugh whenever it was pulled on me. The hustler would call and claim he had a regular trick who was looking for a three-way. The hustler would often add some extravagant promise of travel or outlandish fees. But he'd insist on trying out the goods first. There almost never was a three-way. But you could have some great sex if you wanted to go along for the ride.

It seemed that half the hustlers of San Francisco worked their way through my life by using that ploy. Once I realized what was going on, I simply let it happen and enjoyed it. After all, they were some of the most attractive men in the city, and they were offering me free sex at my convenience.

I also got to know a couple of them, and we did eventually hire one another. It wasn't very common to be hired for a three-way, but it did occur. The other hustlers were also regularly available for sex by themselves. The issue, of course, was that once the relationship moved beyond a professional one, it became an emotional one. No matter how you meet a man, you eventually are going to have to deal with your own and/or his patterns, needs, and wants. A boyfriend is a boyfriend; a fuck buddy is a fuck buddy; a potential lover is always a potential lover. Just be sure what you want, and that it's in line with what the other man is looking for.

Once the word was out that I was hustling, another funny thing happened. I became much more desirable to other men in the bars. It was amazing—the hard-body stars of the places decided that it was a measure of their attractiveness to get a hustler to give it up for free. Men who hadn't thought I was all that interesting before began to be very interested indeed. I was still the same person and still had the same looks, but the way I was approached was altered radically.

You can work this, if you want to. It's a pleasant kind of ego trip, and there can be a bit of vengeance, if you want it. I sometimes pulled S/M numbers on the guys who were newly intrigued with me after having come close to humiliating me with their rejections just a few months earlier. To have a hustler for free is such a big deal in the bar culture that you can start to name your own scene and make your own demands.

Frequency Discounts

I have never been sure about the relatively rare category of frequency discounts, but it did occasionally come up when I was seeing someone with a great deal of regularity and it was fairly obvious that he had limited resources. He would ask for a discount. A regular of any sort is the foundation of your trade. I would never agree to do this with anyone I had seen only a few times; but, if I had seen him at least six times and he asked convincingly, I would make a counteroffer: rather than a discount on the rate for each trick, I would give him a free fuck every sixth time he came by.

When Your Trick Wants to Stop Paying Cash

We have covered two occasions when you will want to consider putting out without a specific cash payment: sugar daddies and barter. There are also the few occasions when you might want to consider a discount. But there are greater problems when your clients begin to believe the fantasy of an intimate relationship with you. They sometimes start to believe your act.

If you spot the dynamic in time, you can finesse it by creating a fictional new lover. (It's always permissible for a hustler to have a lover and talk about him. If it violently turns a trick off, it's probably just as well you found out, since it indicates he will be trouble for you later on.)

The problem will often manifest itself suddenly. One day he simply won't want to pay you. "I thought we'd gone beyond that." You must be firm and tell him no. The sooner, the better; the more emphatically, the kinder. This is your job, and you expect to be paid for it.

For some men, once you talk the problem over with them, it's the actual exchange of cash that bothers them. That's sticky. If you have enough income and if he has the reserves to allow him to take over some of your regular expenditures, you might consider an agreement. Having one guy pay my apartment rent in return for a weekly visit solved the problem for me. This isn't a classic sugar daddy—he's picking only up a few of the tabs—but it's close.

Be especially suspicious of men who "want to take you away from all this." In this world, moralists shouldn't be encouraged.

There's a flip side to this situation. You yourself may become emotionally involved with your customers. You may very well become infatuated with one of them. If you display your affection too obviously, or if you start to give your sex away because you like a man so very much, you may well turn him off. The very idea of paying for it is probably one of his turn-ons, and you're in danger of ruining the scene for him.

Watch yourself in some of these relationships. You are the paid lover. Don't slip and start to act as though you were just another boyfriend. Give presents only to the kindly older men who have made it clear to you that they are primarily buying your companionship and that they would appreciate a gesture of friendship at Christmas time.

Basically, there will be some men who will want to stop paying you, but more would be disenchanted if you lost the mystique of hustling by giving it away.

Pimps

I have never met a gay hustler of any kind who worked with a pimp. I know it happens on the streets of New York and other large cities, but I never even saw it on the streets of Boston. Male hustlers are usually very independent people. I'm inclined to think that pimps are a phenomenon of transvestite and transsexual hustlers who replicate a heterosexual model of prostitution. I also know that some young street hustlers occasionally support a boyfriend, but their situations are markedly different. They have a role-playing relationship with that boyfriend where the hustler, as the source of income, is often playing the "man" of the couple.

The equivalent role of the pimp in gay male hustling may well be that of the agency.

CHAPTER 11
Specialties

You may not need a gimmick, but it doesn't hurt to have one.

There are many specialties; advertising any one of them or a combination can separate your ad from the competition. There are some things to remember, though. If you advertise a specialty, you must be able to deliver with great expertise. Also, remember that a specialty may be too specific. You can attract certain people by its mention; you might also scare away some people who would otherwise be interested.

One answer is to offer numbers of specialties with separate ads. I advertised as an S/M top. That was a valid description of what I could deliver. But I'm also a

161

relatively sophisticated college graduate who knew the best restaurants in town and who could dress appropriately for them. Not many men who were attracted by my self-description as a leather man would call for anything other than some version of S/M. I solved the problem by placing a second ad under a different name promising an escort about town. It didn't bring as much money as the S/M ad, but it was pleasant and worthwhile. If your specialty is too limiting, you should consider similar duo or multiple ads.

Here are some general comments about specialties:

If a trick has only fantasized about certain sex acts, he will often ask for more than he can handle. This is especially true of people who think they are into S/M. They have lived their fantasies in their minds with no check on reality, and when they finally get around to thinking they have to act them out, they go way too far. For example, a man will dream of being beaten with a bullwhip. He will have no experiential basis for what that really feels like. He will give you an extravagant description of the act he thinks he wants to have you perform— the beating—but he just won't know how much it can *hurt*. Once you start in, he's going to want to stop. It will all be much more than he thought it would be.

So, if he says stop, stop. Then reassure him. Make sure he doesn't feel that he's fucked up. This is not the same situation as someone in a bar who has misled you into going home with him and then doesn't want to deliver the goods. This is a man who is paying you good money for his enjoyment. It's part of the high price of his emotional closet that he just didn't know better. Be ready to shift to vanilla sex if he can't handle the specialty when the real thing is actually taking place.

That shift to vanilla sex will happen a great deal. Very often a man will only want the *image* of a fantasy; he won't want the fantasy at all. It was very often more than adequate for me simply to be dressed in leather chaps and vest and boots and to let someone blow me. For many men, that was a sufficiently exotic act that it counted as a S/M scene. Do not assume that anyone expects more than that unless he openly and knowledgeably has negotiated more with you.

People who want to pay for specialties will sometimes not be concerned at all with genital sex. A guy into S/M will ask to clean your apartment. That's all he wants to do: he wants to clean your apartment in the nude while you order him around. Another man into discipline may want only to polish your boots. These men are still paying for your services. They live with their desperate desires, and you are able to free them by letting their dreams happen.

Here are some specific specialties and what you need to live up to them:

S/M

This is the biggest of them all. Since S/M is still something of a taboo subject and people often aren't comfortable seeking it by the usual means—bars, etc.—they will often hire a hustler. The idea of a top also fits many people's concept of a hustler personality in any event. A casual look at hustler ads in a paper will show you how popular S/M is in phone work.

S/M hustlers are almost always strictly top, or at least that's what they tell the world. If you are a bottom, don't advertise the fact. You are inviting the heaviest possible trips and, in most people's minds, will be giving up the right to stop a scene. If you can possibly carry off being a top, do it. It's where the money is, and it's where the safety is.

Don't advertise S/M as a specialty unless you have enough clothes and equipment to convince men that you are an expert and unless you are willing to carry out the role. This is the absolute minimum you will need in terms of attire and toys:

belt or strap
black leather boots
slave collar
rope

handcuffs and/or other wrist restraints and some kind of ankle restraints
candles
clothespins
leather vest
lengths of rawhide or other leather
riding crop
hooks in the wall sufficient for bondage
chaps and/or leather pants
leather jacket
biker cap
hooks in your bedframe or some other way to spread-eagle a trick

If you are really into S/M, you know that this list can go on for a long, long time.

If you are selling S/M, you have to take even more care about the impression of your apartment. Do not think you are going to get someone to lick your boots with gusto if you have a collection of Joan Crawford studio stills on the wall. Something like *Drummer* centerfolds would be a lot more convincing.

Many people I have known thought they had to play an exaggerated macho role from beginning to end while they hustled S/M. On the contrary, there is even more need for you to make the client comfortable. He is more frightened, more in need of emotional support. There will be regulars who will ask you to fulfill a heavy master role on them the next time they see you, but wait for that request before you pull a number on a customer. You need to wear convincing clothing when you greet a customer. I would always have on jeans, boots, and a denim shirt under a leather vest, unless the client had asked specifically for me to be in full leather. Then it would be the whole chaps/jacket/cap outfit. If you don't have full leather, make sure you tell a customer if he inquires; otherwise he will have every reason to feel cheated.

The best hint that he wants you to assume your role immediately is if he calls you "sir" or "master" right from the beginning. Never forget that this customer is more frightened than the others. To some extent, he *wants* to be; the tension is part of the scene for him. Still, be prepared to let him calm down. Go through the whole routine of beer or coffee and conversation. He will let you know if that's going to break his excitement too much.

When you think he has had time to become comfortable enough, you simply ask if he agrees that it's time to begin the scene. He'll ask you how. You reply: "By calling me 'sir' every time you open your mouth." The inevitable response: "Yes, sir." The last step in your opening sequence: "Then start licking my boots." He will be in heaven.

Don't go too far too fast. Basically, the trick wants to experience a few quick parts of S/M. The boots fulfill a need for a touch of humiliation as does saying 'sir.' Play with his tits fairly roughly to give him some pain. At some point you should handcuff him to introduce bondage. Slap his ass, but nothing else unless he indicates his interest. Use a belt very sparingly unless he asks for more. You must let him suck your cock, though you can tease him to great effect about "earning it."

One thing doesn't change: it's still his orgasm you're after, not your own. You are obviously going to prolong the scene too long if you keep his hands secured behind his back and don't let him jerk off. You can solve that to some extent by jerking him off yourself. (Masturbating a client is one thing; you are in danger of breaking your image if you suck him —*unless* you make some clear statement about how you see that as a top trip on him, telling him that you're dragging his orgasm from him, for instance.)

Once he does come, remember that the trip is over. That is untrue only if he has told you specifically that he is capable of multiple orgasms, or if he is someone you know who wants to have a heavy trip that could include enduring a scene even after he has come.

The reality is that most people are only into the *image* of S/M and aren't into very heavy trips. Make sure you don't go too far too soon, or you will lose your clients' trust.

You should leave various pieces of equipment

around the room in plain sight to let him pick up on some options. I used to hang different types of restraints on the wall and leave candles and titclamps out on a tabletop by the bed. Hot-wax trips are very exciting for many customers. I think it's because it's something just exotic enough that they might not have experienced it with a run-of-the-mill bar trick whose idea of S/M is just talking dirty while getting a blowjob. Be sure you don't use beeswax candles, which can cause real damage. Plumber's candles are the best; votive candles from a religious-supply store are perfect and add a certain tingle to the whole concept.

Many men will get off on wearing a slave collar. Make sure you have one open and available. For variety, you can get a collection of dog collars as well.

You will soon learn that many men want to have their bodies shaved. Some will just want their balls shaved; others will want a full neck-down shaving. Make sure you have scissors and old-fashioned safety razors handy—and plenty of shaving cream. If you can afford a hair clipper, get one. It's dramatic when you use it to take off most of the hair, and it makes the rest of the job much easier. Don't think about using a straight razor unless you really know how. Of course, if you do know how, the dramatic use of a strop to sharpen the razor will add a special touch to the scene.

There are many other variations on the theme, but

it's basically up to the customer to let you know what he wants. Unless you get very clear signals otherwise, you should assume the client is after a moderate scene. But you must be prepared to deliver much more if you have advertised specifically. If you are not really into S/M, you will run into trouble. Some people may not think a scene is worth their money if you don't leave marks after a belting or a whipping.

This book isn't meant to be a primer on S/M. There isn't the time or space to go into every one of the major areas of interest and knowledge that are covered by the label. But here are some basics: Don't do anything you are unsure of or in which you are inexperienced. Piercings, very heavy whippings, and complex bondage are all things that call for a great deal of knowledge. Don't experiment blindly with them.

If you are heavily into S/M and have so much equipment that your room has the look of a dungeon or a playroom, make sure you advertise it. It will be a big selling point.

Some special points about S/M hustling:

The phone. While explicit questions about sex are usually a giveaway for jerk-off calls, in most cases, you need to be prepared to answer more detailed questions about S/M than you would respond to in other kinds of hustling.

Age. An S/M hustler can be much older than other

men who sell sex. Being somewhat older can actually be something of a plus, since it can translate into an impression of power and knowledge and safety. I have known guys who were able to be successful hustlers well into their forties if they had a well-equipped game room and full leather. Just be honest about it in your ad and your conversation.

Verbal abuse and other kinds of humiliation. Listen carefully to a trick's words. He'll give you very clear hints as to the level and kind of verbal abuse he wants. Going into a verbal trip that turns you on without knowing that it'll turn him on can be disastrous. There are, for instance, many men who'll hate being called boy or slave just as there are many others who want nothing more in their lives to make them happy.

Bondage. More than anything else, people who answer an ad promising bondage expect great expertise. If you can't out-tie a Boy Scout, don't mention bondage specifically in your ad.

Here are some other specialties:

Military Discipline
If you were in the service or went to a military school or college and know how to bark orders convincingly, advertise it by all means. You will have to have some

semblance of a uniform look, though. Authenticity is important in all specialties; it's essential here. You must have a legitimate military uniform to carry out this scene. You must be extremely neat and clean— that's one of the things that clients will be looking for from you. They will want your apartment to be as well kept as a barracks. You must have short hair, you must have an even better body than you would have to otherwise.

Fisting

If you don't know a lot about fisting, don't advertise it. People who are into this trip can spot a fake a mile away. It can also be downright dangerous if you don't know something about what you're doing.

Getting Fucked

If you advertise getting fucked, you must be clean. Douche before the trick arrives. Warning: if he tells you on the phone he wants it "dirty," he's letting you know he wants a scat scene.

But it's the nineties. Yes, you can reduce your risk of contracting AIDS by using a condom. How much risk do you really want to assume? Getting fucked very frequently is simply not a bright idea in the middle of the epidemic. Condoms *do* break. There are accidents. You can make a decent living without taking this risk. If you crave it, you can still get anal satisfaction from dildos.

Clothing and Footwear

If you advertise a clothing fetish, you must have a very complete wardrobe in your special interest. "Underwear" doesn't mean you have a couple of pair of Jockey shorts. You must have at least two dozen different styles and be prepared to wear them all. The same with boot or shoe fetishes. The people who are interested in this are going to expect many pairs of footwear.

I met one man who had a fetish for Bass Weejuns. He had a room in which he had every possible size of Weejuns. It looked like a well-stocked shoe store. When he hired a hustler, what he really wanted was to give him a pair of perfectly fitted, never-before-worn pair of loafers. Once you put on the shoes, sex could begin.

The man adored these shoes. He would lick them and kiss them passionately once the hustler put them on. He wanted the hustler to step on him so he could feel the new leather on his chest and belly. He was a fanatic.

At the end of every session, the man would not only pay the hustler, he would also give him the shoes. It was part of his greatest pleasure to go shopping later to buy a replacement pair. He was especially pleased when the hustler had an unusual size that made the replacement difficult. There was a thrill in his chase as well as in his capture. Having to have to go all over town to find just the right size, or having to have to contact the factory and have a replacement shipped by overnight freight was part of his pleasure. (He would become demented if there was a gap in his collection. He was always convinced that he would find yet another size 13AA that very night the slot was empty.)

Whatever else you think, the man was happy. He had a good occupation, decent friends, a beautiful apartment, and a very clearly defined way to achieve his sexual outlet. And he paid well—even before you counted in the extra bonus of the new pair of Bass Weejuns.

Escort Services

Escorting goes all the way from being a date for dinner at the Ritz to accompanying someone on a tour of leather bars. Sex is usually expected at some point, but not always. Agree on a price that involves an extended period of time. Make sure you understand just where he wants to go and that you have the clothes to dress appropriately.

Remember that a lot of your appeal is the appeal of being a man living a gay lifestyle. If you are living in a city that is large enough to have them, the client's going to want to go to gay restaurants and clubs. If you offer this service, be prepared to meet your friends with a polyestered Midwesterner beside you.

Fantasies

Many men have fantasies they never intend to live out but which excite them nonetheless. Let's not get into the psychology of sexual repression; let's just deal with the reality.

These men will want to jerk off while you and they talk about their dreamworld, or they are going to want you to talk out their fantasies as well. It's more difficult than it might seem. Picture yourself sitting at your kitchen table talking to a perfectly decent-looking forty-year-old who has just told you about his two kids in college and who is now telling you that he wants to be called a cunt and treated like his version of a cheap woman when you get into the bedroom. The transition can be difficult because the trips can be so outrageous.

Many men will want to act out their dreamworlds. When you trick on your own with a peer, you probably go through a form of courtship. Some key words and symbols will be exchanged beforehand, but the whole process of relating usually includes a progression toward intimacy. Hustling doesn't provide time for such niceties. And, remember, the client thinks he is buying just that intimacy. He is going to tell you bluntly what he wants, and he is going to expect you to deliver a realistic version of it. Even the shyest, least-experienced customer has built up so much energy about finally doing *it*—whatever *it* might be—that usually he will tell you what he wants with only a little prodding. It becomes something like improvisational theater. You are told who you are, and you are now expected to play the part.

It helped me to tell the client that the role began once we entered the bedroom. It allowed me a stage, in effect, that I could act upon. It was up to him to define my character and to give me the clues I needed to know how to satisfy his desires. You must be prepared to go from a calm social setting to a frenzied sexual peak in a matter of moments. You must be willing to produce the facade of sexual caring and performance without any of the props that you are used to having in other social/sexual settings.

Some of the most common fantasies that men will ask for include infantilism (being treated as a baby, diapered, probably spanked). School scenarios are popular—you will be asked to be the teacher who finds some incriminating evidence of the boy's being bad and will be expected to punish him for it. The coach who forces the athlete to work out—demanding more push-ups, demeaning him for his sloppy belly, etc.—is very common. Don't be surprised by any of them.

Getting Shaved
It will absolutely amaze you how many men will want to shave your body. It amazed me. They either

want you to have done it, or they will actually want to do it themselves.

A shaved torso is now a kind of chic thing, though it was very out-of-the-ordinary back when I was hustling in the early seventies. Just walking down the street at a gay street fair or some other occasion when men are going to be shirtless, you can see that many men take a razor to their chests and legs, usually to show off their muscular development. Glance through a selection of gay magazines, and you'll see how many models have trimmed their pubic hair and shave their assholes and their balls.

I'm not sure just how much the custom of shaving the bodies of video stars influenced this fetish; it seems to me that customers were asking for it long before the video explosion. In any event, it becomes a special fetish.

If you do shave your body, make sure you advertise the fact. Even if you shave only your balls, which is the favorite among customers, put it in your ad or make sure you mention it when you are going through your initial telephone negotiation with a prospective customer.

If you don't have a shaved body, you have to decide what it's worth to you to let customers do it. And you should decide how much you want to be paid for each step in the process: your chest, your pubes, the hair around your ass, your legs.

If you are going to be interested in shaving, invest in a pair of clippers. Shaving a hairy chest and hairy legs with just a wet razor can become very time consuming, and the erotic charge will be over long before the task is. A pair of barber's clippers, which you should have anyway for clients who want to be shaved, will be a good investment. You can zip off the major layers of hair, and then you or the client can go over them with a wet razor to get the hairless smoothness desired.

Some words of warning: the hair *does* grow back if you don't keep shaving. The result can be a very itchy and bumpy period of time. In fact, for some men, the process of letting their body hair grow back in can be excruciating. Make sure you consider that before you take it all off cavalierly.

If you do shave your body, you can make it more comfortable for yourself by oiling it liberally. Use baby oil after the shower, before you towel-dry. It will make it much easier on yourself as the hair grows back and it will help keep you from having ingrown hairs that sometimes become annoying, especially when they become infected.

CHAPTER 12
Stretching Your Dollars

There are a few ways to gain a few extra dollars. They can be very tacky, but you might as well know about them.

Beer or Other Alcohol
If the trick asks for beer or alcohol, tell him you have nothing in the house. If he wants a drink or a beer, he should bring it along. If he asks specifically if there's something he can pick up for you at the store, you can always ask for cigarettes, milk, or whatever. Most customers will not take the money they spend off your fee. But, if they do don't argue.

Clothing

If someone mentions a clothing fetish of any kind that relates to anything you are interested in, don't turn him away automatically because you don't have the required items on hand. Jump right in and say, "I could really get into it, but I don't have the stuff here." It may turn out to be something simple like a clean jockstrap that he can pick up on his way over.

Clothing fetishists often find it very exciting to take part in the accumulation of the things that turn them on. I once had a regular who loved underwear. We would go to men's stores and buy different briefs. The very act of being with me while I made my selection could cause him to orgasm if he even touched his cock slightly.

Sex Toys

If someone wants to know if you'll fuck him with a dildo and you don't have one, tell him to buy one and bring it along. If you're into S/M hustling, by the way, and you want to know more about a regular customer's interests, have him present you with a new item to use on each occasion. You'll end up with a remarkable accumulation of titclamps and slave collars.

Sell Your Jockstraps and Jockey Shorts

If you have a customer who refers constantly to your underwear or your jeans or your socks, for that matter, offer to sell them to him for their replacement value.

You can expand this by selling those items through mail-order columns. There's a special added bonus here. While it is true that out-of-town phone calls seldom show up, if you start selling your jocks to someone and let him know you're a hustler, he will very likely seek you out when he comes to town. It will increase his fantasy about you. You will need a post-office box to do this selling, or you'll have lots of weirdos showing up at your doorway.

I first became aware of how lucrative this can be when I was the editor of *The Advocate*. We had a policy of tracking down complaints made by anyone who felt he hadn't gotten good service from our advertisers. One of the worst offenders was a man who offered his dirty underwear. When we contacted him, he assured us that he was trying to keep up with demand; but there had been so many men trying to buy his Jockey shorts who demanded that a load of come be dropped in them that it just hadn't been humanly possible to keep up with demand.

Hustling Others

Once people know you're selling it, some of your friends are going to ask if they can work your phone when you're away. The intrigue will attract them, as will the easy money; and they will want to hustle only occasionally, not often enough to justify their own ad and phone.

Well, you might want to do this once in a while. It's a plus that they will keep your phone answered, and that helps. If you aren't there, even your regulars will assume you're out of the business, so it's good to have someone answering the phone who can assure them that you're just away for a while. Don't take more than a little cut from your friends. Do not try to set up an agency. Not only is it not worth the time and effort, you're going to invite the police to bust you for prostitution, when they might have overlooked a loner.

There's another issue here: you need to have someone on hand who will do three-ways with you. It's a fairly common request. As I've said, if the first-time caller on the phone asks for a three-way, he's probably beating off. But you'll find that your regulars want to watch you and some other guy or have fantasies about having two men at the same time. You should be ready to satisfy them.

Dirty Letters

Can you write easily? Guys will pay money to hear about a hustler's latest exploits. You can just ad a sentence to your hustling ad and offer them a regular subscription to your letters for a set fee—say five dollars per two-page letter. Then you can photocopy them as you want to. There are many, many men out there who will be happy to have intimate correspondence from a hustler.

CHAPTER 13
Photography

Fucking a man in the magazines or one who has modeled for one of the major physique studios is a great gay fantasy. If you want to expand your market of clients, this is by far the best way to do it. The headline "Mandate Centerfold" or "Colt Model" is the most appealing ever. Men will fly across country to get laid by that special guy they just jerked off to in a skin book.

Also, you will often be asked for photographs. A trick will want one as a memento or will ask to purchase one over the phone. Still other men collect hustlers' portraits for their own reasons.

Obviously, there is a vast range of photographic

options. Before you go too far with them, stop and think. Realize that once you've had your photograph printed you have totally committed yourself to an openly gay lifestyle. You will have greatly limited your options, socially and vocationally.

What does it take? There's an easy rule of thumb: you must be exceptional in at least two of three areas:

You must have a very big cock

You must have a very handsome face

You must have an extraordinary body

If you don't have at least two of these assets, don't even bother trying.

If you do want to model, here are your options:

Studios

There are many photographic studios in the country that carry prestige: Colt, Zeus, Falcon are among the best known. You can find their professionally-laid-out ads in nearly every gay publication and just write to the address in the advertisement. You can approach the companies by sending a Polaroid of yourself nude. They will get back to you if they think there is any possibility of using you as a model.

If you pose for a studio, you will most often be paid a very modest amount of money based on the time you spend in front of the camera. The studios are increasing their involvement in hard-core porn, especially with the video revolution, so you'll probably be expected to fuck and suck on camera. Different studios have different standards of payment, but you'll seldom make money that will be worth it by itself.

Your photographs will not only be sold by themselves via mail order and through the studio's catalogs and magazines, they will also be used in gay skin magazines, where the company trades use of photography for advertising space.

You must always remember this: *the photographer makes money from the photographs, not the model.* Once you are in a studio's stable of models, you might get an expense-paid trip to do a location shooting, but it's more likely that modeling will cost you money. The biggest studios are in New York, Los Angeles, and San Francisco. If you want to interview with them, you can wait until their representative has a reason to visit your hometown, but more likely you'll have to pay out your own money to travel to their offices.

Is it ever worthwhile? *Yes.* if you are in the business of hustling for the long run, it is definitely worthwhile to have your photographs appear in calendars, cards, and magazines. There will be nothing else that will advance your name recognition and make men interested in seeing you so much as modeling. It is just that the cycles of when photographs are printed and then published are out of your hands, and they will take a long time to be reprinted regularly. Once they do, you will be very well rewarded with enthusiastic calls from your fans.

Magazines

Being on the cover of *Advocate Men* or the centerfold of *Mandate* or spread on the pages of one of the other big gay magazines is a big plus for a hustler. You can apply directly to the editor or art director listed on the publication's masthead with the same kind of Polaroid you used for the studios. If you don't live in New York, Los Angeles, or wherever the magazine's headquarters are located, the magazine can sometimes refer you to a photographer who lives closer to you. You will be paid almost nothing to be photographed nude in the magazine.

A few hints:

Magazines will make up a fictitious name for you unless you specifically request otherwise. You will have to be forceful about using your hustling name to get it printed in a magazine.

It will take months for your picture to be published. If you were a stunningly handsome man who posed for a brilliant photographer who produced shots that were perfect for the next issue of a magazine, it would still take at least four months for the photos to appear on the newsstands. Depending on many editorial factors, it can easily take a year.

You will have no control over the ways the photos will be used. Before any photographer starts your session, he will hand you a model release to sign. It will totally give away all your rights on how the pictures can be used. You will not be allowed to restrict the photographer's use in any way. Your butt can show up in calendars, in advertisements, on greeting cards and you'll have nothing to say about it. You will earn no more money because of it.

Independent Photographers

Every city seems to have photographers who take male nudes at some professional level. You can approach these guys yourself. With an independent photographer, you have an option: you can reverse the usual process of payment and hire him to take your photographs. It will cost a fair amount of money, but you can then be the person who offers the photographs to a magazine you choose, and you are the one who has shouldered the risk that the payment will be sufficient to cover expenses and perhaps make a small profit. Make sure you explain your intent to the photographer, though. What you are after is a "buyout"—not just prints—and a professional will demand to have a special contract for that.

Most people don't realize that they are buying only prints when they hire a photographer—not publication rights, nor the negatives that will be necessary to secure publication. Make sure you don't set yourself up for a big disappointment or a huge bill when you do sell photographs to magazines.

Remember though, that it will take a long time for you to recoup your money even if the photographs are sold. Almost all gay magazines pay for photography on the basis of the size of the reproduced image and the type of image—black and white or color. You should have both taken so you can meet different needs, though most magazines use only color now. Those local publications that are printed on newsprint are still a market for black-and-white photography. (Local publications also are a way to avoid the problem of very long waits for pictures to appear in national magazines. Many of the regional newspapers can have your image out there in a matter of weeks, even days.) They won't be as prestigious as one of the national publications, but they can give you a start. The magazines pay on publication— that is, they pay when the photographs appear in an issue on the newsstand.

There's another advantage to having control of the photographer's product. You can sell individual prints to your customers, or you can offer them yourself through the mail.

If you do want to model, here are some little pieces of advice:

A tan is usually essential.

You will have to pose with a hard-on or a half-hard-on.

Don't wear tight clothes just before your photo shoot. Especially avoid belts or elastic-banded underwear for a couple of hours before the session. Their imprint will show in the image.

When you look at yourself in the mirror to see if you think you have what it takes, remember that the camera will tend to make you look heavier than you actually are.

Very well defined muscles will overcome a small cock in photographs. But only an *enormous* prick will overcome a lack of definition.

CHAPTER 14
Some Realities

The Law

Before you turn your first trick, go see a lawyer. If you are working the phone on your own, you are not likely to attract police attention, but you never know. You need the lawyer on the chance that you might be busted. You don't want his advice on how to go about your business—and the attorney probably wouldn't want to be involved in any event—but you want him to be there if you are arrested. The very presence of a lawyer can affect how the police decide to charge you.

A lawyer can also tell you what are the basic operating procedures in your city. It might be that you should always have a small amount of cash on hand to post bond in a night court.

If you think you are too embarrassed to talk to a lawyer now, think how you would feel calling him up as a stranger from jail.

Taxes

There's another legal problem that you must consider. Your income is undeclared cash. You could conceivably not pay income taxes. That is probably not wise. It can look suspicious if you disappear completely from the tax rolls and you may regret not paying into Social Security sometime in the future. You can pay taxes on at least some of your income, claiming to be a social escort, for instance. But watch out. If you do this, then no other money can ever go through your bank account or in any other way leave a paper trail that the IRS would ever be able to find. And be aware that you are in much more danger from the IRS if you file a false income-tax return than for anything else. See an accountant. This is a real issue you are going to have to deal with, and you should have some solid advice. Most local gay publications advertise accountants who should be willing to work with you to figure out how to finesse this problem.

Telling People What You Do

People tend to have a misconception about how much they can control information about themselves. No matter how much you insist on discretion or defend your right to privacy, once they learn, people are going to spread the word that you are selling it. Even if it weren't true, you might as well face the fact that you should tell some people, you will want to tell others, and it will change your relationships when you do let the word get around.

If you don't tell people who know you that you are hustling, you will end up with a very embarrassed man at your door. Go back over the list of the types of men who hire hustlers, and you'll see that it's a pretty catholic group. You know people who pay for sex, you just don't know which of your friends are included in the group.

At first, you'll be a little embarrassed to tell people you're hustling. Some very few will be judgmental; most will be titillated.

The image of being a hustler is going to dramatically increase your sexual attractiveness. Men in the bars are going to want to have the prestige of having a hustler for free. It will be a great boost for your ego. Never hustle in a gay bar, though. Always turn down an offer of money in any place where you are well known. You'll be eighty-sixed very quickly.

There is one thing that will happen in a few relationships that is depressing. Friends will be very defensive that you are hustling them. They will question themselves about buying you a beer they automatically would have offered you before. They will simply trust you less. It's not going to be the case all the time, but it will happen.

CHAPTER 15
Why You Shouldn't Do It

You have heard only advice and encouragement from me so far, but there are many good reasons *not* to hustle. You should examine them carefully. They essentially revolve around time limitations. You only can hustle for a short time before you get tired of it, and not very long before you're too old.

Hustling makes sense as an occupation "in between." It is a way to work through school, spend a year in San Francisco, travel, read, pursue an art or a craft. It can never be viewed as a life's work. You can fantasize about writing the great book about hustling, but you are never going to live off that. Nor is it likely that some great knight on a white charger is going to come along and want to pay your bills for you after you are done hustling.

Here are some of the problems about hustling:

Money

You are going to be dealing with an uncontrollable cash income. It begins to stop feeling like the salary you've come to expect from work. It's like Monopoly money. You'll spend it too easily. You have $200 in your pocket and you can't put it into a bank account because you can't explain it to the IRS, so why not buy new CDs? At least try to discipline yourself to put some part of each trick's fee aside for a rainy day.

False Relationships

You are constantly offering up illusions of intimacy. It is a problem to be living with that lack of veracity; it is also a problem when a relationship with a client develops. You will like some of your customers emotionally and socially. When you or the other person tries to alter the foundation that your friendship or your affair has been built upon—your hustling—someone could be hurt and disappointed, and it could be you.

How Do You Explain Your Time?

Okay, you leave your job and go to San Francisco and hustle for a couple of years. It's over. You want your job back. What are you going to tell the personnel officer you have been doing for those two years?

It's Boring

It can be very, very boring to sit and wait for the phone to ring, especially once you realize how seldom the call is going to bring a real trick in any event. I just hope you enjoy reading or watching the soaps.

Your Lover's Going to Hate It

Maybe two hustlers can establish an understanding relationship, but even that is often difficult. It's very likely going to bother anyone you try to relate to if you hustle. Even if the idea of your hustling doesn't bother him, the demands on your time and the insistent phone ringing will get to him.

You Might Get Arrested and You Might Go to Jail

You just might.

You've heard of the writers
but didn't know where to find them

Samuel R. Delany • Pat Califia • Carol Queen • Lars Eighner • Felice Picano • Lucy Taylor • Aaron Travis • Michael Lassell • Red Jordan Arobateau • Michael Bronski • Tom Roche • Maxim Jakubowski • Michael Perkins • Camille Paglia • John Preston • Laura Antoniou • Alice Joanou • Cecilia Tan • Michael Perkins • Tuppy Owens • Trish Thomas • Lily Burana • Alison Tyler • Marco Vassi • Susie Bright • Randy Turoff • Allen Ellenzweig • Shar Rednour

You've seen the sexy images
but didn't know where to find them

Robert Chouraqui • Charles Gatewood • Richard Kern • Eric Kroll • Vivienne Maricevic • Housk Randall • Barbara Nitke • Trevor Watson • Mark Avers • Laura Graff • Michele Serchuk • Laurie Leber • John Willie • Sylvia Plachy • Romain Slocombe • Robert Mapplethorpe • Doris Kloster

You can find them all in
Masquerade

a publication designed expressly for the connoisseur of the erotic arts.

ORDER TODAY
SAVE 50%
1 year (6 issues) for $15; 2 years (12 issues) for only $25!

Essential. —*Skin Two*

The best newsletter I have ever seen!
—*Secret International*

Very informative and enticing.
—*Redemption*

A professional, insider's look at the world of erotica. —*Screw*

I recommend a subscription to **MASQUERADE**... It's good stuff.
—*Black Sheets*

MASQUERADE presents some of the best articles on erotica, fetishes, sex clubs, the politics of porn and every conceivable issue of sex and sexuality.
—*Factsheet Five*

Fabulous. —*Tuppy Owens*

MASQUERADE is absolutely lovely ... marvelous images.
—*Le Boudoir Noir*

Highly recommended. —*Eidos*

DIRECT

Masquerade/Direct • DEPT BMBB17 • 801 Second Avenue • New York, NY 10017 • FAX: 212.986.7355
MC/VISA orders can be placed by calling our toll-free number: 800.375.2356

☐ PLEASE SEND ME A 1 YEAR SUBSCRIPTION FOR $30 *NOW* $15!
☐ PLEASE SEND ME A 2 YEAR SUBSCRIPTION FOR $60 *NOW* $25!

NAME _____

ADDRESS _____

CITY _____ STATE _____ ZIP _____

TEL (___) _____

PAYMENT: ☐ CHECK ☐ MONEY ORDER ☐ VISA ☐ MC

CARD # _____ EXP. DATE _____

No C.O.D. orders. Please make all checks payable to Masquerade/Direct. Payable in U.S. currency only.

MASQUERADE BOOKS

MASQUERADE

ATAULLAH MARDAAN
KAMA HOURI/DEVA DASI
$7.95/512-3
Two legendary tales of the East in one spectacular volume. *Kama Houri* details the life of a sheltered Western woman who finds herself living within the confines of a harem—where she discovers herself thrilled with the extent of her servitude. *Deva Dasi* is a tale dedicated to the cult of the Dasis—the sacred women of India who devoted their lives to the fulfillment of the senses—while revealing the sexual rites of Shiva.

"...memorable for the author's ability to evoke India present and past.... Mardaan excels in crowding her pages with the sights and smells of India, and her erotic descriptions are convincingly realistic."
—Michael Perkins,
The Secret Record: Modern Erotic Literature

J. P. KANSAS
ANDREA AT THE CENTER
$6.50/498-4
Kidnapped! Lithe and lovely young Andrea is whisked away to a distant retreat. Gradually, she is introduced to the ways of the Center, and soon becomes quite friendly with its other inhabitants—all of whom are learning to abandon restraint in their pursuit of the deepest sexual satisfaction. This tale of the ultimate sexual training facility is a nationally bestselling title and a classic of modern erotica.

VISCOUNT LADYWOOD
GYNECOCRACY
$9.95/511-5
An infamous story of female domination returns to print. Julian, whose parents feel he shows just a bit too much spunk, is sent to a very special private school, in hopes that he will learn to discipline his wayward soul. Once there, Julian discovers that his program of study has been devised by the deliciously stern Mademoiselle de Chambonnard. In no time, Julian is learning the many ways of pleasure—under the firm hand of this demanding headmistress.

CHARLOTTE ROSE, EDITOR
THE 50 BEST PLAYGIRL FANTASIES
$6.50/460-7
A steamy selection of women's fantasies straight from the pages of *Playgirl*—the leading magazine of sexy entertainment for women. These tales of seduction—specially selected by no less an authority than Charlotte Rose, author of such bestselling women's erotica as *Women at Work* and *The Doctor is In*—are sure to set your pulse racing. From the innocent to the insatiable, these women let no fantasy go unexplored.

N. T. MORLEY
THE PARLOR
$6.50/496-8
Lovely Kathryn gives in to the ultimate temptation. The mysterious John and Sarah ask her to be their slave—an idea that turns Kathryn on so much that she can't refuse! But who are these two mysterious strangers? Little by little, Kathryn not only learns to serve, but comes to know the inner secrets of her stunning keepers.

J. A. GUERRA, EDITOR
**COME QUICKLY:
FOR COUPLES ON THE GO**
$6.50/461-5
The increasing pace of daily life is no reason to forgo a little carnal pleasure whenever the mood strikes. Here are over sixty of the hottest fantasies around—all designed to get you going in less time than it takes to dial 976. A super-hot volume especially for couples on a modern schedule.

ERICA BRONTE
LUST, INC.
$6.50/467-4
Lust, Inc. explores the extremes of passion that lurk beneath even the coldest, most business-like exteriors. Join in the sexy escapades of a group of high-powered professionals whose idea of office decorum is like nothing you've ever encountered! Business attire not required....

VANESSA DURIES
THE TIES THAT BIND
$6.50/510-7
The incredible confessions of a thrillingly unconventional woman. From the first page, this chronicle of dominance and submission will keep you gasping with its vivid depictions of sensual abandon. At the hand of Masters Georges, Patrick, Pierre and others, this submissive seductress experiences pleasures she never knew existed....

M. S. VALENTINE
THE CAPTIVITY OF CELIA
$6.50/453-4
Colin is mistakenly considered the prime suspect in a murder, forcing him to seek refuge with his cousin, Sir Jason Hardwicke. In exchange for Colin's safety, Jason demands Celia's unquestioning submission—knowing she will do anything to protect her lover. Sexual extortion!

AMANDA WARE
BINDING CONTRACT
$6.50/491-7
Louise was responsible for bringing many prestigious clients into Claremont's salon—so he was more than willing to have her miss a little work in order to pleasure one of his most important customers. But Eleanor Cavendish had her mind set on something more rigorous than a simple wash and set. Sexual slavery!

BUY ANY 4 BOOKS & CHOOSE 1 ADDITIONAL BOOK, OF EQUAL OR LESSER VALUE, AS YOUR FREE GIFT

MASQUERADE BOOKS

BOUND TO THE PAST
$6.50/452-6
Anne accepts a research assignment in a Tudor mansion. Upon arriving, she finds herself aroused by James, a descendant of the mansion's owners. Together they uncover the perverse desires of the mansion's long-dead master—desires that bind Anne inexorably to the past—not to mention the bedpost!

SACHI MIZUNO
SHINJUKU NIGHTS
$6.50/493-3
A tour through the lives and libidos of the seductive East. No one is better that Sachi Mizuno at weaving an intricate web of sensual desire, wherein many characters are ensnared and enraptured by the demands of their long-denied carnal natures.

PASSION IN TOKYO
$6.50/454-2
Tokyo—one of Asia's most historic and seductive cities. Come behind the closed doors of its citizens, and witness the many pleasures that await. Lusty men and women from every stratum of Japanese society free themselves of all inhibitions....

MARTINE GLOWINSKI
POINT OF VIEW
$6.50/433-X
With the assistance of her new, unexpectedly kinky lover, she discovers and explores her exhibitionist tendencies—until there is virtually nothing she won't do before the horny audiences her man arranges! Unabashed acting out for the sophisticated voyeur.

RICHARD McGOWAN
A HARLOT OF VENUS
$6.50/425-9
A highly fanciful, epic tale of lust on Mars! Cavortia—the most famous and sought-after courtesan in the cosmopolitan city of Venus—finds love and much more during her adventures with some of the most remarkable characters in recent erotic fiction.

M. ORLANDO
THE ARCHITECTURE OF DESIRE
Introduction by Richard Manton.
$6.50/490-9
Two novels in one special volume! In *The Hotel Justine*, an elite clientele is afforded the opportunity to have any and all desires satisfied. *The Villa Sin* is inherited by a beautiful woman who soon realizes that the legacy of the ancestral estate includes bizarre erotic ceremonies.

CHET ROTHWELL
KISS ME, KATHERINE
$5.95/410-0
Beautiful Katherine can hardly believe her luck. Not only is she married to the charming and oh-so-agreeable Nelson, she's free to live out all her erotic fantasies with other men. Katherine's desires are more than any one man can handle.

MARCO VASSI
THE STONED APOCALYPSE
$5.95/401-1/mass market
"Marco Vassi is our champion sexual energist."—VLS
During his lifetime, Marco Vassi praised by writers as diverse as Gore Vidal and Norman Mailer, and his reputation was worldwide. *The Stoned Apocalypse* is Vassi's autobiography; chronicling a cross-country trip on America's erotic byways, it offers a rare glimpse of a generation's sexual imagination.

ROBIN WILDE
TABITHA'S TICKLE
$6.50/468-2
Tabitha's back! The story of this vicious vixen—and her torturously tantalizing cohorts—didn't end with *Tabitha's Tease*. Once again, many men fall under the spell of scrumptious co-eds and find themselves enslaved to demands and desires they never dreamed existed. Think it's a man's world? Guess again. With Tabitha around, no man gets what he wants until she's completely satisfied—and, maybe, not even then....

TABITHA'S TEASE
$5.95/387-2
When poor Robin arrives at The Valentine Academy, he finds himself subject to the torturous teasing of Tabitha—the Academy's most notoriously domineering co-ed. But Tabitha is pledge-mistress of a secret sorority dedicated to enslaving young men. Robin finds himself the utterly helpless (and wildly excited) captive of Tabitha & Company's weird desires! A marathon of ticklish torture!

ERICA BRONTE
PIRATE'S SLAVE
$5.95/376-7
Lovely young Erica is stranded in a country where lust knows no bounds. Desperate to escape, she finds herself trading her firm, luscious body to any and all men willing and able to help her. Her adventure has its ups and downs, ins and outs—all to the undeniable pleasure of lusty Erica!

CHARLES G. WOOD
HELLFIRE
$5.95/358-9
A vicious murderer is running amok in New York's sexual underground—and Nick O'Shay, a virile detective with the NYPD, plunges deep into the case. He soon becomes embroiled in an elusive world of fleshly extremes, hunting a madman seeking to purge America with fire and blood sacrifices. Set in New York's infamous sexual underground.

CLAIRE BAEDER, EDITOR
LA DOMME: A DOMINATRIX ANTHOLOGY
$5.95/366-X
A steamy smorgasbord of female domination! Erotic literature has long been filled with heartstopping portraits of domineering women, and now the most memorable have been brought together in one beautifully brutal volume. A must for all fans of true Woman Power.

MASQUERADE BOOKS

CHARISSE VAN DER LYN
SEX ON THE NET
$5.95/399-6
Electrifying erotica from one of the Internet's hottest and most widely read authors. Encounters of all kinds—straight, lesbian, dominant/submissive and all sorts of extreme passions—are explored in thrilling detail.

STANLEY CARTEN
NAUGHTY MESSAGE
$5.95/333-3
Wesley Arthur discovers a lascivious message on his answering machine. Aroused beyond his wildest dreams by the acts described, Wesley becomes obsessed with tracking down the woman behind the seductive voice. His search takes him through strip clubs, sex parlors and no-tell motels—and finally to his randy reward....

AKBAR DEL PIOMBO
DUKE COSIMO
$4.95/3052-0
A kinky romp played out against the boudoirs, bathrooms and ballrooms of the European nobility, who seem to do nothing all day except each other. The lifestyles of the rich and licentious are revealed in all their glory.

A CRUMBLING FAÇADE
$4.95/3043-1
The return of that incorrigible rogue, Henry Pike, who continues his pursuit of sex, fair or otherwise, in the most elegant homes of the most debauched aristocrats.

CAROLE REMY
FANTASY IMPROMPTU
$6.50/513-1
A mystical, musical journey into the deepest recesses of a woman's soul. Kidnapped and held in a remote island retreat, Chantal—a renowned erotic writer—finds herself catering to every sexual whim of the mysterious and arousing Bran. Bran is determined to bring Chantal to a full embracing of her sensual nature, even while revealing himself to be something far more than human....

BEAUTY OF THE BEAST
$5.95/332-5
A shocking tell-all, written from the point-of-view of a prize-winning reporter. And what reporting she does! All the secrets of an uninhibited life are revealed, and each lusty tableau is painted in glowing colors.

DAVID AARON CLARK
THE MARQUIS DE SADE'S JULIETTE
$4.95/240-X
The Marquis de Sade's infamous Juliette returns—and emerges as the most perverse and destructive nightstalker modern New York will ever know. One by one, the innocent are drawn in by Juliette's empty promise of immortality, only to fall prey to her strange and deadly lusts.

ANONYMOUS
NADIA
$5.95/267-1
Follow the delicious but neglected Nadia as she works to wring every drop of pleasure out of life—despite an unhappy marriage. A classic title providing a peek into the secret sexual lives of another time and place.

NIGEL McPARR
THE TRANSFORMATION OF EMILY
$6.50/519-0
The shocking story of Emily Johnson, live-in domestic. Without warning, Emily finds herself dismissed by her mistress, and sent to serve at Lilac Row—the home of Charles and Harriet Godwin. In no time, Harriet has Emily doing things she'd never dreamed would be required of her—all involving the erotic discipline Harriet imposes with relish. Little does Emily realize that, as strict and punishing as Harriet Godwin is, nothing could compare to the rigors of her next "position..."

THE STORY OF A VICTORIAN MAID
$5.95/241-8
What were the Victorians really like? Chances are, no one believes they were as stuffy as their Queen, but who would have imagined such unbridled libertines!

TITIAN BERESFORD
CINDERELLA
$6.50/500-X
Beresford triumphs again with this intoxicating tale, filled with castle dungeons and tightly corseted ladies-in-waiting, naughty viscounts and impossibly cruel masturbatrixes—nearly every conceivable method of erotic torture is explored and described in lush, vivid detail.

JUDITH BOSTON
$6.50/525-5
Young Edward would have been lucky to get the stodgy old companion he thought his parents had hired for him. Instead, an exquisite woman arrives at his door, and Edward finds his lewd behavior never goes unpunished by the unflinchingly severe Judith Boston! Together they take the downward path to perversion!

NINA FOXTON
$5.95/443-7
An aristocrat finds herself bored by run-of-the-mill amusements for "ladies of good breeding." Instead of taking tea with proper gentlemen, naughty Nina "milks" them of their most private essences. No man ever says "No" to Nina!

P. N. DEDEAUX
THE NOTHING THINGS
$5.95/404-6
Beta Beta Rho—highly exclusive and widely honored—has taken on a new group of pledges. The five women will be put through the most grueling of ordeals, and punished severely for any shortcomings—much to everyone's delight!

BUY ANY 4 BOOKS & CHOOSE 1 ADDITIONAL BOOK, OF EQUAL OR LESSER VALUE, AS YOUR FREE GIFT

MASQUERADE BOOKS

LYN DAVENPORT
THE GUARDIAN II
$6.50/505-0
The tale of Felicia Brookes—the lovely young woman held in submission by the demanding Sir Rodney Wentworth—continues in this volume of sensual surprises. No sooner has Felicia come to love Rodney than she discovers that she must now accustom herself to the guardianship of the debauched Duke of Smithton. Surely Rodney will rescue her from the domination of this stranger. *Won't he?*

DOVER ISLAND
$5.95/384-8
Dr. David Kelly has planted the seeds of his dream— a Corporal Punishment Resort. Soon, many people from varied walks of life descend upon this isolated retreat, intent on fulfilling their every desire. Including Marcy Harris, the perfect partner for the lustful Doctor....

THE GUARDIAN
$5.95/371-6
Felicia grew up under the tutelage of the lash—and she learned her lessons well. Sir Rodney Wentworth has long searched for a woman capable of fulfilling his cruel desires, and after learning of Felicia's talents, sends for her. Felicia discovers that the "position" offered her is delightfully different than anything she could have expected!

LIZBETH DUSSEAU
THE APPLICANT
$6.50/501-8
"Adventuresome young women who enjoys being submissive sought by married couple in early forties. Expect no limits." Hilary answers an ad, hoping to find someone who can meet her special needs. The beautiful Liza turns out to be a flawless mistress, and together with her husband, Oliver, she trains Hilary to be the perfect servant.

ANTHONY BOBARZYNSKI
STASI SLUT
$4.95/3050-4
Adina lives in East Germany, where she can only dream about the freedoms of the West. But then she meets a group of ruthless and corrupt STASI agents. They use her body for their own perverse gratification, while she opts to use her talents and attractions in a final bid for total freedom!

JOCELYN JOYCE
PRIVATE LIVES
$4.95/309-0
The lecherous habits of the illustrious make for a sizzling tale of French erotic life. A widow has a craving for a young busboy; he's sleeping with a rich businessman's wife; her husband is minding his sex business elsewhere! Sexual entanglements run through this tale of upper crust lust!

SARAH JACKSON
SANCTUARY
$5.95/318-X
Sanctuary explores both the unspeakable debauchery of court life and the unimaginable privations of monastic solitude, leading the voracious and the virtuous on a collision course that brings history to throbbing life.

THE WILD HEART
$4.95/3007-5
A luxury hotel is the setting for this artful web of sex, desire, and love. A newlywed sees sex as a duty, while her hungry husband tries to awaken her to its tender joys. A Parisian entertains wealthy guests for the love of money. Each episode provides a new variation in this lusty Grand Hotel!

LOUISE BELHAVEL
FRAGRANT ABUSES
$4.95/88-2
The saga of Clara and Iris continues as the now-experienced girls enjoy themselves with a new circle of worldly friends whose imaginations match their own. Perversity follows the lusty ladies around the globe!

SARA H. FRENCH
MASTER OF TIMBERLAND
$5.95/327-9
A tale of sexual slavery at the ultimate paradise resort. One of our bestselling titles, this trek to Timberland has ignited passions the world over—and stands poised to become one of modern erotica's legendary tales.

MARY LOVE
MASTERING MARY SUE
$5.95/351-1
Mary Sue is a rich nymphomaniac whose husband is determined to declare her mentally incompetent and gain control of her fortune. He brings her to a castle where, to Mary Sue's delight, she is unleashed for a veritable sex-fest!

THE BEST OF MARY LOVE
$4.95/3099-7
Mary Love leaves no coupling untried and no extreme unexplored in these scandalous selections from *Mastering Mary Sue, Ecstasy on Fire, Vice Park Place, Wanda,* and *Naughtier at Night.*

AMARANTHA KNIGHT
THE DARKER PASSIONS: THE PICTURE OF DORIAN GRAY
$6.50/342-2
Amarantha Knight takes on Oscar Wilde, resulting in a fabulously decadent tale of highly personal changes. One young man finds his most secret desires laid bare by a portrait far more revealing than he could have imagined....

THE DARKER PASSIONS READER
$6.50/432-1
The best moments from Knight's phenomenally popular Darker Passions series. Here are the most eerily erotic passages from her acclaimed sexual reworkings of *Dracula, Frankenstein, Dr. Jekyll & Mr. Hyde* and *The Fall of the House of Usher.*

THE DARKER PASSIONS: THE FALL OF THE HOUSE OF USHER
$6.50/528-X
The Master and Mistress of the house of Usher indulge in every form of decadence, and initiate their guests into the many pleasures to be found in utter submission.

MASQUERADE BOOKS

THE DARKER PASSIONS:
DR. JEKYLL AND MR. HYDE
$4.95/227-2
It is a story of incredible transformations achieved through mysterious experiments. Explore the steamy possibilities of a tale where no one is quite who—or what—they seem. Victorian bedrooms explode with hidden demons!

THE DARKER PASSIONS: FRANKENSTEIN
$5.95/248-5
What if you could create a living human? What shocking acts could it be taught to perform, to desire? Find out what pleasures await those who play God....

THE DARKER PASSIONS: DRACULA
$5.95/326-0
The infamous erotic retelling of the Vampire legend. "Well-written and imaginative, Amarantha Knight gives fresh impetus to this myth, taking us through the sexual and sadistic scenes with details that keep us reading.... A classic in itself has been added to the shelves." —Divinity

---

THE PAUL LITTLE LIBRARY
PECULIAR PASSIONS OF LADY MEG/ LOVE SLAVE
$8.95/529-8/Trade paperback
Two classics from modern erotica's most popular author! What are the sexy secrets *Lady Meg* hides? What are the appetites that lurk beneath the surface of this irresistible vixen? What does it take to be the perfect instrument of pleasure—or go about acquiring a willing *Love Slave* of one's own? Paul Little spares no detail!

THE BEST OF PAUL LITTLE
$6.50/469-0
Known throughout the world for his fantastic portrayals of punishment and pleasure, Little never fails to push readers over the edge of sensual excitement.

ALL THE WAY
$6.95/509-3
Two excruciating novels from Paul Little in one hot volume! *Going All the Way* features an unhappy man who tries to purge himself of the memory of his lover with a series of quirky and uninhibited lovers. *Pushover* tells the story of a serial spanker and his celebrated exploits.

THE DISCIPLINE OF ODETTE
$5.95/334-1
Odette's was sure marriage would rescue her from her family's "corrections." To her horror, she discovers that her beloved has also been raised on discipline. A shocking erotic coupling.

THE PRISONER
$5.95/330-9
Judge Black has built a secret room below a penitentiary, where he sentences the prisoners to hours of exhibition and torment while his friends watch. Judge Black's House of Corrections is equipped with one purpose in mind: to administer his own brand of rough justice!

TEARS OF THE INQUISITION
$4.95/146-2
The incomparable Paul Little delivers a staggering account of pleasure and punishment. "There was a tickling inside her as her nervous system reminded her she was ready for sex. But before her was...the Inquisitor!"

DOUBLE NOVEL
$4.95/86-6
The Metamorphosis of Lisette Joyaux tells the story of a young woman initiated into an incredible world world of lesbian lusts. *The Story of Monique* reveals the twisted sexual rituals that beckon the ripe and willing Monique.

CHINESE JUSTICE AND OTHER STORIES
$4.95/153-5
The story of the excruciating pleasures and delicious punishments inflicted on foreigners under the leaders of the Boxer Rebellion. Each woman is brought before the authorities and grilled, to the delight of their perverse captors.

CAPTIVE MAIDENS
$5.95/440-2
Three beautiful young women find themselves powerless against the debauched landowners of 1824 England. They are banished to a sexual slave colony, and corrupted by every imaginable perversion.

SLAVE ISLAND
$5.95/441-0
A leisure cruise is waylaid by Lord Henry Philbrock, a sadistic genius. The ship's passengers are kidnapped and spirited to his island prison, where the women are trained to accommodate the most bizarre sexual cravings of the rich, the famous, the pampered and the perverted.

ALIZARIN LAKE
SEX ON DOCTOR'S ORDERS
$5.95/402-X
Beth, a nubile young nurse, uses her considerable skills to further medical science by offering incomparable and insatiable assistance in the gathering of important specimens. Soon, an assortment of randy characters is lending a hand in this highly erotic work.

THE EROTIC ADVENTURES OF HARRY TEMPLE
$4.95/127-6
Harry Temple's memoirs chronicle his amorous adventures from his initiation at the hands of insatiable sirens, through his stay at a house of hot repute, to his encounters with a chastity-belted nympho!

JOHN NORMAN
TARNSMAN OF GOR
$6.95/486-0
This controversial series returns! Tarl Cabot is transported to Gor. He must quickly accustom himself to the ways of this world, including the caste system which exalts some as Priest-Kings or Warriors, and debases others as slaves. A spectacular world unfolds in this first volume of John Norman's Gorean series.

BUY ANY 4 BOOKS & CHOOSE 1 ADDITIONAL BOOK, OF EQUAL OR LESSER VALUE, AS YOUR FREE GIFT

MASQUERADE BOOKS

OUTLAW OF GOR
$6.95/487-9
In this second volume, Tarl Cabot returns to Gor, where he might reclaim both his woman and his role of Warrior. But upon arriving, he discovers that his name, his city and the names of those he loves have become unspeakable. Cabot has become an outlaw, and must discover his new purpose on this strange planet, where danger stalks the outcast, and even simple answers have their price....

PRIEST-KINGS OF GOR
$6.95/488-9
Tarl Cabot searches for the truth about his lovely wife Talena. Does she live, or was she destroyed by the mysterious, all-powerful Priest-Kings? Cabot is determined to find out—even while knowing that no one who has approached the mountain stronghold of the Priest-Kings has ever returned alive....

NOMADS OF GOR
$6.95/527-1
Another provocative trip to the barbaric and mysterious world of Gor. Norman's heroic Tarnsman finds his way across this Counter-Earth, pledged to serve the Priest-Kings in their quest for survival. Unfortunately for Cabot, his mission leads him to the savage Wagon People—nomads who may very well kill before surrendering any secrets....

RACHEL PEREZ

AFFINITIES
$4.95/113-6
"Kelsy had a liking for cool upper-class blondes, the long-legged girls from Lake Forest and Winnetka who came into the city to cruise the lesbian bars on Halsted, looking for breathless ecstasies...." A scorching tale of lesbian libidos unleashed, from a writer more than capable of exploring every nuance of female passion in vivid detail.

SYDNEY ST. JAMES

RIVE GAUCHE
$5.95/317-1
The Latin Quarter, Paris, circa 1920. Expatriate bohemians couple with abandon—before eventually abandoning their ambitions amidst the intoxicating temptations waiting to be indulged in every bedroom.

GARDEN OF DELIGHT
$4.95/3058-X
A vivid account of sexual awakening that follows an innocent but insatiably curious young woman's journey from the furtive, forbidden joys of dormitory life to the unabashed carnality of the wild world.

DON WINSLOW

THE FALL OF THE ICE QUEEN
$6.50/520-4
She was the most exquisite of his courtiers: the beautiful, aloof woman whom Rahn the Conqueror chose as his Consort. But the regal disregard with which she treated Rahn was not to be endured. It was decided that she would submit to his will, and learn to serve her lord in the fashion he had come to expect. And as so many knew, Rahn's depraved expectations have made his court infamous....

PRIVATE PLEASURES
$6.50/504-2
An assortment of sensual encounters designed to appeal to the most discerning reader. Frantic voyeurs, licentious exhibitionists, and everyday lovers are here displayed in all their wanton glory—proving again that fleshly pleasures have no more apt chronicler than Don Winslow.

THE INSATIABLE MISTRESS OF ROSEDALE
$6.50/494-1
The story of the perfect couple: Edward and Lady Penelope, who reside in beautiful and mysterious Rosedale manor. While Edward is a true connoisseur of sexual perversion, it is Lady Penelope whose mastery of complete sexual pleasure makes their home infamous. Indulging one another's bizarre whims is a way of life for this wicked couple, and none who encounter the extravagances of Rosedale will forget what they've learned....

SECRETS OF CHEATEM MANOR
$6.50/434-8
Edward returns to his late father's estate, to find it being run by the majestic Lady Amanda. Edward can hardly believe his luck—Lady Amanda is assisted by her two beautiful, lonely daughters, Catherine and Prudence. What the randy young man soon comes to realize is the love of discipline that all three beauties share.

KATERINA IN CHARGE
$5.95/409-7
When invited to a country retreat by a mysterious couple, two randy young ladies can hardly resist! But do they have any idea what they're in for? Whatever the case, the imperious Katerina will make her desires known very soon—and demand that they be fulfilled... Sexual innocence subjugated and defiled.

THE MANY PLEASURES OF IRONWOOD
$5.95/310-3
Seven lovely young women are employed by The Ironwood Sportsmen's Club, where their natural talents are put to creative use. A small and exclusive club with seven carefully selected sexual connoisseurs, Ironwood is dedicated to the relentless pursuit of sensual pleasure.

CLAIRE'S GIRLS
$5.95/442-9
You knew when she walked by that she was something special. She was one of Claire's girls, a woman carefully dressed and groomed to fill a role, to capture a look, to fit an image crafted by the sophisticated proprietress of an exclusive escort agency. High-class whores blow the roof off in this blow-by-blow account of life behind the closed doors of a sophisticated brothel.

N. WHALLEN

TAU'TEVU
$6.50/426-7
In a mysterious land, the statuesque and beautiful Vivian learns to subject herself to the hand of a mysterious man. He systematically helps her prove her own strength, and brings to life in her an unimagined sensual fire. But who is this man, who goes only by the name of Orpheo?

MASQUERADE BOOKS

COMPLIANCE
$5.95/356-2
Fourteen stories exploring the pleasures of ultimate release. Characters from all walks of life learn to trust in the skills of others, hoping to experience the thrilling liberation of sexual submission. Here are the many joys to be found in some of the most forbidden sexual practices around....

THE CLASSIC COLLECTION
PROTESTS, PLEASURES, RAPTURES
$5.95/400-3
Invited for an allegedly quiet weekend at a country vicarage, a young woman is stunned to find herself surrounded by shocking acts of sexual sadism. Soon, her curiosity is piqued, and she begins to explore her own capacities for cruelty. The ultimate tale of a woman's erotic awakening.

THE YELLOW ROOM
$5.95/378-3
The "yellow room" holds the secrets of lust, lechery, and the lash. There, bare-bottomed, spread-eagled, and open to the world, demure Alice Darvell soon learns to love her lickings. In the second tale, hot heiress Rosa Coote and her lusty servants whip up numerous adventures in punishment and pleasure.

SCHOOL DAYS IN PARIS
$5.95/325-2
The rapturous chronicles of a well-spent youth! Few Universities provide the profound and pleasurable lessons one learns in after-hours study—particularly if one is young and available, and lucky enough to have Paris as a playground. A stimulating look at the pursuits of young adulthood.

MAN WITH A MAID
$4.95/307-4
The adventures of Jack and Alice have delighted readers for eight decades! A classic of its genre, Man with a Maid tells an outrageous tale of desire, revenge, and submission. This tale qualifies as one of the world's most popular adult novels—with over 200,000 copies in print!

CONFESSIONS OF A CONCUBINE III: PLEASURE'S PRISONER
$5.95/357-0
Filled with pulse-pounding excitement—including a daring escape from the harem and an encounter with an unspeakable sadist—Pleasure's Prisoner adds an unforgettable chapter to this thrilling confessional.

CLASSIC EROTIC BIOGRAPHIES
JENNIFER
$4.95/107-1
The return of one of the Sexual Revolution's most notorious heroines. From the bedroom of a notoriously insatiable dancer to an uninhibited young ashram, Jennifer traces the exploits of one thoroughly modern woman as she lustfully explores the limits of her own sexuality.

JENNIFER III
$5.95/292-2
The further adventures of erotica's most daring heroine. Jennifer has a photographer's eye for details—particularly of the masculine variety! One by one, her subjects submit to her demands for sensual pleasure, becoming part of her now-infamous gallery of erotic conquests.

RHINOCEROS

KATHLEEN K.
SWEET TALKERS
$6.95/516-6
Kathleen K. ran a phone-sex company in the late 80s, and she opens up her diary for a very thought provoking peek at the life of a phone-sex operator. Transcripts of actual conversations are included.

"If you enjoy eavesdropping on explicit conversations about sex... this book is for you." —Spectator

"Highly recommended." —Shiny International
Trade /$12.95/192-6

THOMAS S. ROCHE
DARK MATTER
$6.95/484-4
"Dark Matter is sure to please gender outlaws, body-mod vampires, goth vampires, boys who wish they were dykes, and anybody who's not to sure where the fine line should be drawn between pleasure and pain. It's a handful." —Pat Califia

"Here is the erotica of the cumming millenium.... You will be deliciously disturbed, but never disappointed." —Poppy Z. Brite

NOIROTICA: AN ANTHOLOGY OF EROTIC CRIME STORIES
$6.95/390-2
A collection of darkly sexy tales, taking place at the crossroads of the crime and erotic genres. Thomas S. Roche has gathered together some of today's finest writers of sexual fiction, all of whom explore the murky terrain where desire runs irrevocably afoul of the law.

ROMY ROSEN
SPUNK
$6.95/492-5
Casey, a lovely model poised upon the verge of super-celebrity, falls for an insatiable young rock singer—not suspecting that his sexual appetite has led him to experiment with a dangerous new aphrodisiac. Casey becomes an addict, and her craving plunges her into a strange underworld, where the only chance for redemption lies with a shadowy young man with a secret of his own.

BUY ANY 4 BOOKS & CHOOSE 1 ADDITIONAL BOOK, OF EQUAL OR LESSER VALUE, AS YOUR FREE GIFT

MASQUERADE BOOKS

MOLLY WEATHERFIELD
CARRIE'S STORY
$6.95/485-2
"I had been Jonathan's slave for about a year when he told me he wanted to sell me at an auction. I wasn't in any condition to respond when he told me this..." Desire and depravity run rampant in this story of uncompromising mastery and irrevocable submission. A unique piece of erotica that is both thoughtful and hot!

"I was stunned by how well it was written and how intensely foreign I found its sexual world.... And, since this is a world I don't frequent... I thoroughly enjoyed the National Geo tour." —bOING bOING

"Hilarious and harrowing... just when you think things can't get any wilder, they do." —Black Sheets

CYBERSEX CONSORTIUM
CYBERSEX: THE PERV'S GUIDE TO FINDING SEX ON THE INTERNET
$6.95/471-2
You've heard the objections: cyberspace is soaked with sex. Okay—so where is it!? Tracking down the good stuff—the real good stuff—can waste an awful lot of expensive time, and frequently leave you high and dry. The Cybersex Consortium presents an easy-to-use guide for those intrepid adults who know what they want. No horny hacker can afford to pass up this map to the kinkiest rest stops on the Info Superhighway.

AMELIA G, EDITOR
BACKSTAGE PASSES
$6.95/438-0
Amelia G, editor of the goth-sex journal *Blue Blood*, has brought together some of today's most irreverent writers, each of whom has outdone themselves with an edgy, antic tale of modern lust. Punks, metalheads, and grunge-trash roam the pages of *Backstage Passes*, and no one knows their ways better...

GERI NETTICK WITH BETH ELLIOT
MIRRORS: PORTRAIT OF A LESBIAN TRANSSEXUAL
$6.95/435-6
The alternately heartbreaking and empowering story of one woman's long road to full selfhood. Born a male, Geri Nettick knew something just didn't fit. And even after coming to terms with her own gender dysphoria—and taking steps to correct it—she still fought to be accepted by the lesbian feminist community to which she felt she belonged. A fascinating, true tale of struggle and discovery.

DAVID MELTZER
UNDER
$6.95/290-0
The story of a 21st century sex professional living at the bottom of the social heap. After surgeries designed to increase his physical allure, corrupt government forces drive the cyber-gigolo underground—where even more bizarre cultures await him.

ORF
$6.95/110-1
He is the ultimate musician-hero—the idol of thousands, the fevered dream of many more. And like many musicians before him, he is misunderstood, misused—and totally out of control. Every last drop of feeling is squeezed from a modern-day troubadour and his lady love.

LAURA ANTONIOU, EDITOR
NO OTHER TRIBUTE
$6.95/294-9
A collection sure to challenge Political Correctness in a way few have before, with tales of women kept in bondage to their lovers by their deepest passions. Love pushes these women beyond acceptable limits, rendering them helpless to deny anything to the men and women they adore. A volume dedicated to all Slaves of Desire.

SOME WOMEN
$6.95/300-7
Over forty essays written by women actively involved in consensual dominance and submission. Professional mistresses, lifestyle leatherdykes, whipmakers, titleholders—women from every conceivable walk of life lay bare their true feelings about explosive issues.

BY HER SUBDUED
$6.95/281-7
These tales all involve women in control—of their lives, their lovers, their men. So much in control that they can remorselessly break rules to become powerful goddesses of the men who sacrifice all to worship at their feet.

TRISTAN TAORMINO & DAVID AARON CLARK, EDITORS
RITUAL SEX
$6.95/391-0
While many people believe the body and soul to occupy almost completely independent realms, the many contributors to *Ritual Sex* know—and demonstrate—that the two share more common ground than society feels comfortable acknowledging. From personal memoirs of ecstatic revelation, to fictional quests to reconcile sex and spirit, *Ritual Sex* provides an unprecedented look at private life.

TAMMY JO ECKHART
PUNISHMENT FOR THE CRIME
$6.95/427-5
Peopled by characters of rare depth, these stories explore the true meaning of dominance and submission. From an encounter between two of society's most despised individuals, to the explorations of longtime friends, these tales take you where few others have ever dared....

AMARANTHA KNIGHT, EDITOR
SEDUCTIVE SPECTRES
$6.95/464-X
Breathtaking tours through the erotic supernatural via the macabre imaginations of today's best writers. Never before have ghostly encounters been so alluring, thanks to a cast of otherworldly characters well-acquainted with the pleasures of the flesh.

MASQUERADE BOOKS

SEX MACABRE
$6.95/392-9
Horror tales designed for dark and sexy nights. Amarantha Knight—the woman behind the Darker Passions series—has gathered together erotic stories sure to make your skin crawl, and heart beat faster.

FLESH FANTASTIC
$6.95/352-X
Humans have long toyed with the idea of "playing God": creating life from nothingness, bringing life to the inanimate. Now Amarantha Knight collects stories exploring not only the act of Creation, but the lust that follows....

GARY BOWEN
DIARY OF A VAMPIRE
$6.95/331-7
"Gifted with a darkly sensual vision and a fresh voice, [Bowen] is a writer to watch out for."
—Cecilia Tan

Rafael, a red-blooded male with an insatiable hunger for the same, is the perfect antidote to the effete malcontents haunting bookstores today. The emergence of a bold and brilliant vision, rooted in past and present.

RENÉ MAIZEROY
FLESHLY ATTRACTIONS
$6.95/299-X
Lucien was the son of the wantonly beautiful actress, Marie-Rose Hardanges. When she decides to let a "friend" introduce her son to the pleasures of love, Marie-Rose could not have foretold the excesses that would lead to her own ruin and that of her cherished son.

JEAN STINE
THRILL CITY
$6.95/411-9
Thrill City is the seat of the world's increasing depravity, and this classic novel transports you there with a vivid style you'd be hard pressed to ignore. No writer is better suited to describe the extremes of this modern Babylon.

SEASON OF THE WITCH
$6.95/268-X
"A future in which it is technically possible to transfer the total mind...of a rapist killer into the brain dead but physically living body of his female victim. Remarkable for intense psychological technique. There is eroticism but it is necessary to mark the differences between the sexes and the subtle altering of a man into a woman." —The Science Fiction Critic

GRANT ANTREWS
ROGUES GALLERY
$6.95/522-8
A stirring evocation of dominant/submissive love. Two doctors meet and slowly fall in love. Once Beth reveals her hidden desires to Jim, the two explore the forbidden acts that will come to define their distinctly exotic affair.

MY DARLING DOMINATRIX
$6.95/447-X
When a man and a woman fall in love, it's supposed to be simple and uncomplicated—unless that woman happens to be a dominatrix. Curiosity gives way to desire in this story of one man's awakening to the joys of willing slavery.

JOHN WARREN
THE TORQUEMADA KILLER
$6.95/367-8
Detective Eva Hernandez gets her first "big case": a string of vicious murders taking place within New York's SM community. Eva assembles the evidence, revealing a picture of a world misunderstood and under attack—and gradually comes to understand her own place within it.

THE LOVING DOMINANT
$6.95/218-3
Everything you need to know about an infamous sexual variation—and an unspoken type of love. Warren guides readers through this world and reveals the too-often hidden basis of the D/S relationship: care, trust and love.

LAURA ANTONIOU WRITING AS "SARA ADAMSON"
THE TRAINER
$6.95/249-3
The Marketplace includes not only willing slaves, but the exquisite trainers who take submissives firmly in hand. And now these mentors divulge the desires that led them to become the ultimate figures of authority.

THE SLAVE
$6.95/173-X
The second volume in the "Marketplace" trilogy. One talented submissive longs to join the ranks of those who have proven themselves worthy of entry into the Marketplace. But the delicious price is high....

THE MARKETPLACE
$6.95/3096-2
The volume that introduced the Marketplace to the world—and established it as one of the most popular realms in contemporary SM fiction.

DAVID AARON CLARK
SISTER RADIANCE
$6.95/215-9
Rife with Clark's trademark vivisections of contemporary desires, sacred and profane. The vicissitudes of lust and romance are examined against a backdrop of urban decay in this testament to the allure of the forbidden.

THE WET FOREVER
$6.95/117-9
The story of Janus and Madchen—a small-time hood and a beautiful sex worker on the run from one of the most dangerous men they have ever known—examines themes of loyalty, sacrifice, redemption and obsession amidst Manhattan's sex parlors and underground S/M clubs.

BUY ANY 4 BOOKS & CHOOSE 1 ADDITIONAL BOOK, OF EQUAL OR LESSER VALUE, AS YOUR FREE GIFT

MASQUERADE BOOKS

MICHAEL PERKINS
EVIL COMPANIONS
$6.95/3067-9
Set in New York City during the tumultuous waning years of the Sixties, *Evil Companions* has been hailed as "a frightening classic." A young couple explores the nether reaches of the erotic unconscious in a shocking confrontation with the extremes of passion.

THE SECRET RECORD: MODERN EROTIC LITERATURE
$6.95/3039-3
Michael Perkins surveys the field with authority and unique insight. Updated and revised to include the latest trends, tastes, and developments in this misunderstood and maligned genre.

AN ANTHOLOGY OF CLASSIC ANONYMOUS EROTIC WRITING
$6.95/140-3
Michael Perkins has collected the very best passages from the world's erotic writing. "Anonymous" is one of the most infamous bylines in publishing history—and these steamy excerpts show why! Includes excerpts from some of the most famous titles in the history of erotic literature.

LIESEL KULIG
LOVE IN WARTIME
$6.95/3044-X
Madeleine knew that the handsome SS officer was a dangerous man, but she was just a cabaret singer in Nazi-occupied Paris, trying to survive in a perilous time. When Josef fell in love with her, he discovered that a beautiful woman can sometimes be as dangerous as any warrior.

HELEN HENLEY
ENTER WITH TRUMPETS
$6.95/197-7
Helen Henley was told that women just don't write about sex—much less the taboos she was so interested in exploring. So Henley did it alone, flying in the face of "tradition" by writing this touching tale of arousal and devotion in one couple's kinky relationship.

ALICE JOANOU
BLACK TONGUE
$6.95/258-2
"Joanou has created a series of sumptuous, brooding, dark visions of sexual obsession, and is undoubtedly a name to look out for in the future."
—Redeemer

Exploring lust at its most florid and unsparing, *Black Tongue* is a trove of baroque fantasies—each redolent of forbidden passions. Joanou creates some of erotica's most mesmerizing and unforgettable characters.

TOURNIQUET
$6.95/3060-1
A heady collection of stories and effusions from the pen of one our most dazzling young writers. Strange tales abound, from the story of the mysterious and cruel Cybele, to an encounter with the sadistic entertainment of a bizarre after-hours cafe. A complex and riveting series of meditations on desire.

CANNIBAL FLOWER
$4.95/72-6
The provocative debut volume from this acclaimed writer.
"She is waiting in her darkened bedroom, as she has waited throughout history, to seduce the men who are foolish enough to be blinded by her irresistible charms...., She is the goddess of sexuality, and *Cannibal Flower* is her haunting siren song."
—Michael Perkins

PHILIP JOSÉ FARMER
A FEAST UNKNOWN
$6.95/276-0
"Sprawling, brawling, shocking, suspenseful, hilarious..."
—Theodore Sturgeon
Farmer's supreme anti-hero returns. "I was conceived and born in 1888." Slowly, Lord Grandrith—armed with the belief that he is the son of Jack the Ripper—tells the story of his remarkable and unbridled life. His story begins with his discovery of the secret of immortality—and progresses to encompass the furthest extremes of human behavior.

THE IMAGE OF THE BEAST
$6.95/166-7
Herald Childe has seen Hell, glimpsed its horror in an act of sexual mutilation. Childe must now find and destroy an inhuman predator through the streets of a polluted and decadent Los Angeles of the future. One clue after another leads Childe to an inescapable realization about the nature of sex and evil....

DANIEL VIAN
ILLUSIONS
$6.95/3074-1
Two tales of danger and desire in Berlin on the eve of WWII. From private homes to lurid cafés, passion is exposed in stark contrast to the brutal violence of the time, as desperate people explore their deepest, darkest sexual desires.

SAMUEL R. DELANY
THE MAD MAN
$8.99/408-9
"Reads like a pornographic reflection of Peter Ackroyd's *Chatterton* or A. S. Byatt's *Possession*.... Delany develops an insightful dichotomy between [his protagonist]'s two worlds: the one of cerebral philosophy and dry academia, the other of heedless, 'impersonal' obsessive sexual extremism. When these worlds finally collide...the novel achieves a surprisingly satisfying resolution...." —*Publishers Weekly*

For his thesis, graduate student John Marr researches the life of Timothy Hasler: a philosopher whose career was cut tragically short over a decade earlier. On another front, Marr finds himself increasingly drawn toward shocking, depraved sexual entanglements with the homeless men of his neighborhood, until it begins to seem that Hasler's death might hold some key to his own life as a gay man in the age of AIDS. Unquestionably one of Delany's most shocking works, *The Mad Man* is one of American erotic literature's most transgressive titles.

MASQUERADE BOOKS

EQUINOX
$6.95/157-8
The Scorpion has sailed the seas in a quest for every possible pleasure. Her crew is a collection of the young, the twisted, the insatiable. A drifter comes into their midst and is taken on a fantastic journey to the darkest, most dangerous sexual extremes—until he is finally a victim to their boundless appetites. An early title that set the way for the author's later explorations of extreme, forbidden sexual behaviors. Long out of print, this disturbing tale is finally available under the author's original title.

ANDREI CODRESCU
THE REPENTANCE OF LORRAINE
$6.95/329-5
"One of our most prodigiously talented and magical writers."
—NYT Book Review
By the acclaimed author of *The Hole in the Flag* and *The Blood Countess*. An aspiring writer, a professor's wife, a secretary, gold anklets, Maoists, Roman harlots—and more—swirl through this spicy tale of a harried quest for a mythic artifact. Written when the author was a young man, this lusty yarn was inspired by the heady days of the Sixties. Includes a new introduction by the author, detailing the events that inspired *Lorraine*'s creation. A touching, arousing product from a more innocent time.

TUPPY OWENS
SENSATIONS
$6.95/3081-4
Tuppy Owens tells the unexpurgated story of the making of *Sensations*—the first big-budget sex flick. Originally commissioned to appear in book form after the release of the film in 1975, *Sensations* is finally released under Masquerade's stylish Rhinoceros imprint.

SOPHIE GALLEYMORE BIRD
MANEATER
$6.95/103-9
Through a bizarre act of creation, a man attains the "perfect" lover—by all appearances a beautiful, sensuous woman, but in reality something far darker. Once brought to life she will accept no mate, seeking instead the prey that will sate her hunger for vengeance.

LEOPOLD VON SACHER-MASOCH
VENUS IN FURS
$6.95/3089-X
This classic 19th century novel is the first uncompromising exploration of the dominant/submissive relationship in literature. The alliance of Severin and Wanda epitomizes Sacher-Masoch's dark obsession with a cruel, controlling goddess and the urges that drive the man held in her thrall. This special edition includes the letters exchanged between Sacher-Masoch and Emilie Mataja, an aspiring writer he sought to cast as the avatar of the forbidden desires expressed in his most famous work.

BADBOY

MIKE FORD, EDITOR
BUTCH BOYS
$6.50/523-9
A big volume of tales dedicated to the rough-and-tumble type who can make a man weak at the knees. From bikers to "gymbos," these no-nonsense studs know just what they want and how to go about getting it. Some of today's best erotic writers explore the many possible variations on the age-old fantasy of the dominant man.

WILLIAM J. MANN, EDITOR
GRAVE PASSIONS
$6.50/405-4
A collection of the most chilling tales of passion currently being penned by today's most provocative gay writers. Unnatural transformations, otherworldly encounters, and deathless desires make for a collection sure to keep readers up late at night—for a variety of reasons!

J. A. GUERRA, EDITOR
COME QUICKLY: FOR BOYS ON THE GO
$6.50/413-5
Here are over sixty of the hottest fantasies around—all designed to get you going in less time than it takes to dial 976. Julian Anthony Guerra, the editor behind the phenomenally popular *Men at Work* and *Badboy Fantasies*, has put together this volume especially for you—a busy man on a modern schedule, who still appreciates a little old-fashioned action.

JOHN PRESTON
HUSTLING: A GENTLEMAN'S GUIDE TO THE FINE ART OF HOMOSEXUAL PROSTITUTION
$6.50/517-4
The very first guide to the gay world's most infamous profession. John Preston solicited the advice and opinions of "working boys" from across the country in his effort to produce the ultimate guide to the hustler's world. Hustling covers every practical aspect of the business, from clientele and payment options to "specialties," sidelines and drawbacks. No stone is left unturned—and no wrong turn left unadmonished—in this guidebook to the ins and outs of this much-mythologized trade.

"...Unrivaled. For any man even vaguely contemplating going into business this tome has got to be the first port of call."
—*Divinity*

"Fun and highly literary. What more could you expect form such an accomplished activist, author and editor?"
—*Drummer*
Trade $12.95/137-3

BUY ANY 4 BOOKS & CHOOSE 1 ADDITIONAL BOOK, OF EQUAL OR LESSER VALUE, AS YOUR FREE GIFT

MASQUERADE BOOKS

MR. BENSON
$4.95/3041-5
Jamie is an aimless young man lucky enough to encounter Mr. Benson. He is soon led down the path of erotic enlightenment, learning to accept this man as his master. Jamie's incredible adventures never fail to excite—especially when the going gets rough! One of the first runaway best-sellers in gay erotic literature.

TALES FROM THE DARK LORD
$5.95/323-6
A new collection of twelve stunning works from the man *Lambda Book Report* called "the Dark Lord of gay erotica." The relentless ritual of lust and surrender is explored in all its manifestations in this heart-stopping triumph of authority and vision from the Dark Lord!

TALES FROM THE DARK LORD II
$4.95/176-4
The second volume of John Preston's masterful short stories. Includes an interview with the author, and a sexy screenplay written for pornstar Scott O'Hara.

THE ARENA
$4.95/3083-0
There is a place on the edge of fantasy where every desire is indulged with abandon. Men go there to unleash beasts, to let demons roam free, to abolish all limits. At the center of each tale are the men who serve there, who offer themselves for the consummation of any passion, whose own bottomless urges compel their endless subservience.

THE HEIR•THE KING
$4.95/3048-2
The ground-breaking novel *The Heir*, written in the lyric voice of the ancient myths, tells the story of a world where slaves and masters create a new sexual society. This edition also includes a completely original work, *The King*, the story of a soldier who discovers his monarch's most secret desires. A special double volume.

THE MISSION OF ALEX KANE

SWEET DREAMS
$4.95/3062-8
It's the triumphant return of gay action hero Alex Kane! In *Sweet Dreams*, Alex travels to Boston where he takes on a street gang that stalks gay teenagers. Mighty Alex Kane wreaks a fierce and terrible vengeance on those who prey on gay people everywhere!

GOLDEN YEARS
$4.95/3069-5
When evil threatens the plans of a group of older gay men, Kane's got the muscle to take it head on. Along the way, he wins the support—and very specialized attentions—of a cowboy plucked right out of the Old West. But Kane and the Cowboy have a surprise waiting for them....

DEADLY LIES
$4.95/3076-8
Politics is a dirty business and the dirt becomes deadly when a political smear campaign targets gay men. Who better to clean things up than Alex Kane?! Alex comes to protect the dreams, and lives, of gay men imperiled by lies and deceit.

STOLEN MOMENTS
$4.95/3098-9
Houston's evolving gay community is victimized by a malicious newspaper editor who is more than willing to sacrifice gays on the altar of circulation. He never counted on Alex Kane, fearless defender of gay dreams and desires.

SECRET DANGER
$4.95/111-X
Homophobia: a pernicious social ill not confined by America's borders. Alex Kane and the faithful Danny are called to a small European country, where a group of gay tourists is being held hostage by ruthless terrorists. Luckily, the Mission of Alex Kane stands as firm foreign policy.

LETHAL SILENCE
$4.95/125-X
The Mission of Alex Kane thunders to a conclusion. Chicago becomes the scene of the right-wing's most noxious plan—facilitated by unholy political alliances. Alex and Danny head to the Windy City to take up battle with the mercenaries who would squash gay men underfoot.

MATT TOWNSEND

SOLIDLY BUILT
$6.50/416-X
The tale of the tumultuous relationship between Jeff, a young photographer, and Mark, the butch electrician hired to wire Jeff's new home. For Jeff, it's love at first sight; Mark, however, has more than a few hang-ups. Soon, both are forced to reevaluate their outlooks, and are assisted by a variety of hot men....

JAY SHAFFER

SHOOTERS
$5.95/284-1
No mere catalog of random acts, *Shooters* tells the stories of a variety of stunning men and the ways they connect in sexual and non-sexual ways. A virtuoso storyteller, Shaffer always gets his man.

ANIMAL HANDLERS
$4.95/264-7
In Shaffer's world, each and every man finally succumbs to the animal urges deep inside. And if there's any creature that promises a wild time, it's a beast who's been caged for far too long. Shaffer has one of the keenest eyes for the nuances of male passion.

FULL SERVICE
$4.95/150-0
Wild men build up steam until they finally let loose. No-nonsense guys bear down hard on each other as they work their way toward release in this finely detailed assortment of masculine fantasies. One of gay erotica's most insightful chroniclers of male passion.

D. V. SADERO

IN THE ALLEY
$4.95/144-6
Hardworking men—from cops to carpenters—bring their own special skills and impressive tools to the most satisfying job of all: capturing and breaking the male sexual beast. Hot, incisive and way over the top

MASQUERADE BOOKS

SCOTT O'HARA
DO-IT-YOURSELF PISTON POLISHING
$6.50/489-5
Longtime sex-pro Scott O'Hara draws upon his acute powers of seduction to lure you into a world of hard, horny men long overdue for a tune-up. Pretty soon, you'll pop your own hood for the servicing you know you need....

SUTTER POWELL
EXECUTIVE PRIVILEGES
$6.50/383-X
No matter how serious or sexy a predicament his characters find themselves in, Powell conveys the sheer exuberance of their encounters with a warm humor rarely seen in contemporary gay erotica.

GARY BOWEN
WESTERN TRAILS
$6.50/477-1
A wild roundup of tales devoted to life on the lone prairie. Gary Bowen—a writer well-versed in the Western genre—has collected the very best contemporary cowboy stories. Some of gay literature's brightest stars tell the sexy truth about the many ways a rugged stud found to satisfy himself—and his buddy—in the Very Wild West.

MAN HUNGRY
$5.95/374-0
By the author of *Diary of a Vampire*. A riveting collection of stories from one of gay erotica's new stars. Dipping into a variety of genres, Bowen crafts tales of lust unlike anything being published today.

KYLE STONE
HOT BAUDS 2
$6.50/479-8
Another collection of cyberfantasies—compiled by the inimitable Kyle Stone. After the success of the original *Hot Bauds*, Stone conducted another heated search through the world's randiest bulletin boards, resulting in one of the most scalding follow-ups ever published. Here's all the scandalous stuff you've heard so much about—sexy, shameless, and eminently user-friendly.

FIRE & ICE
$5.95/297-3
A collection of stories from the author of the infamous adventures of PB 500. Randy, powerful, and just plain bad, Stone's characters always promise one thing: enough hot action to burn away your desire for anyone else....

HOT BAUDS
$5.95/285-0
The author of *Fantasy Board* and *The Initiation of PB 500* combed cyberspace for the hottest fantasies of the world's horniest hackers. Stone has assembled the first collection of the raunchy erotica so many gay men cruise the Information Superhighway for.

FANTASY BOARD
$4.95/212-4
The author of the scalding sci-fi adventures of PB 500 explores the more foreseeable future—through the intertwined lives (and private parts) of a collection of randy computer hackers. On the Lambda Gate BBS, every hot and horny male is in search of a little virtual satisfaction—and is certain to find even more than he'd hoped for!

THE CITADEL
$4.95/198-5
The sequel to *The Initiation of PB 500*. Having proven himself worthy of his stunning master, Micah—now known only as '500'—will face new challenges and hardships after his entry into the forbidding Citadel. Only his master knows what awaits—and whether Micah will again distinguish himself as the perfect instrument of pleasure....

THE INITIATION OF PB 500
$4.95/141-1
He is a stranger on their planet, unschooled in their language, and ignorant of their customs. But this man, Micah—now known only by his number—will soon be trained in every last detail of erotic personal service. And, once nurtured and transformed into the perfect physical specimen, he must begin proving himself worthy of the master who has chosen him....

RITUALS
$4.95/168-3
Via a computer bulletin board, a young man finds himself drawn into a series of sexual rites that transform him into the willing slave of a mysterious stranger. Gradually, all vestiges of his former life are thrown off, and he learns to live for his Master's touch....

ROBERT BAHR
SEX SHOW
$4.95/225-6
Luscious dancing boys. Brazen, explicit acts. Unending stimulation. Take a seat, and get very comfortable, because the curtain's going up on a show no discriminating appetite can afford to miss.

JASON FURY
THE ROPE ABOVE, THE BED BELOW
$4.95/269-8
The irresistible Jason Fury returns—this time, telling the tale of a vicious murderer preying upon New York's go-go boy population. No one is who or what they seem, and in order to solve this mystery and save lives, each studly suspect must lay bare his soul—and more!

ERIC'S BODY
$4.95/151-9
Meet Jason Fury: blond, blue-eyed and up for anything. Fury's sexiest tales are collected in book form for the first time. Follow the irresistible Jason through sexual adventures unlike any you have ever read....

BUY ANY 4 BOOKS & CHOOSE 1 ADDITIONAL BOOK, OF EQUAL OR LESSER VALUE, AS YOUR FREE GIFT

MASQUERADE BOOKS

1 800 906-HUNK

THE connection for hot handfuls of eager guys! No credit card needed—so call now for access to the hottest party line available. Spill it all to bad boys from across the country! (Must be over 18.) Pick one up now.... $3.98 per min.

LARS EIGHNER

WHISPERED IN THE DARK
$5.95/286-8
A volume demonstrating Eighner's unique combination of strengths: poetic descriptive power, an unfailing ear for dialogue, and a finely tuned feeling for the nuances of male passion.

AMERICAN PRELUDE
$4.95/170-5
Eighner is widely recognized as one of our best, most exciting gay writers. He is also one of gay erotica's true masters—and *American Prelude* shows why. Wonderfully written, blisteringly hot tales of all-American lust.

B.M.O.C.
$4.95/3077-6
In a college town known as "the Athens of the Southwest," studs of every stripe are up all night—studying, naturally. Relive university life the way it was supposed to be, with a cast of handsome honor students majoring in Human Homosexuality.

DAVID LAURENTS, EDITOR

SOUTHERN COMFORT
$6.50/466-6
Editor David Laurents now unleashes a collection of tales focusing on the American South—reflecting not only Southern literary tradition, but the many contributions the region has made to the iconography of the American Male.

WANDERLUST:
HOMOEROTIC TALES OF TRAVEL
$5.95/395-3
A volume dedicated to the special pleasures of faraway places. Gay men have always had a special interest in travel—and not only for the scenic vistas. Wanderlust celebrates the freedom of the open road, and the allure of men who stray from the beaten path....

THE BADBOY BOOK OF EROTIC POETRY
$5.95/382-1
Over fifty of today's best poets. Erotic poetry has long been the problem child of the literary world—highly creative and provocative, but somehow too frank to be "literature." Both learned and stimulating, *The Badboy Book of Erotic Poetry* restores eros to its rightful place of honor in contemporary gay writing.

AARON TRAVIS

BIG SHOTS
$5.95/448-8
Two fierce tales in one electrifying volume. In *Beirut*, Travis tells the story of ultimate military power and erotic subjugation; *Kip*, Travis' hypersexed and sinister take on film noir, appears in unexpurgated form for the first time.

EXPOSED
$4.95/126-8
A volume of shorter Travis tales, each providing a unique glimpse of the horny gay male in his natural environment! Cops, college jocks, ancient Romans—even Sherlock Holmes and his loyal Watson—cruise these pages, fresh from the throbbing pen of one of our hottest authors.

BEAST OF BURDEN
$4.95/105-5
Five ferocious tales. Innocents surrender to the brutal sexual mastery of their superiors, as taboos are shattered and replaced with the unwritten rules of masculine conquest. Intense, extreme—and totally Travis.

IN THE BLOOD
$5.95/283-3
Written when Travis had just begun to explore the true power of the erotic imagination, these stories laid the groundwork for later masterpieces. Among the more rewarding rarities included in this volume: "In the Blood" —a heart-pounding descent into sexual vampirism, written with the furious erotic power that is Travis' trademark.

THE FLESH FABLES
$4.95/243-4
One of Travis' best collections. *The Flesh Fables* includes "Blue Light," his most famous story, as well as other masterpieces that established him as the erotic writer to watch. And watch carefully, because Travis always buries a surprise somewhere beneath his scorching detail....

SLAVES OF THE EMPIRE
$4.95/3054-7
"A wonderful mythic tale. Set against the backdrop of the exotic and powerful Roman Empire, this wonderfully written novel explores the timeless questions of light and dark in male sexuality. The locale may be the ancient world, but these are the slaves and masters of our time...." —John Preston

BOB VICKERY

SKIN DEEP
$4.95/265-5
So many varied beauties no one will go away unsatisfied. No tantalizing morsel of manflesh is overlooked—or left unexplored! Beauty may be only skin deep, but a handful of beautiful skin is a tempting proposition.

JR

FRENCH QUARTER NIGHTS
$5.95/337-6
Sensual snapshots of the many places where men get down and dirty—from the steamy French Quarter to the steam room at the old Everard baths. These are nights you'll wish would go on forever....

TOM BACCHUS

RAHM
$5.95/315-5
The imagination of Tom Bacchus brings to life an extraordinary assortment of characters, from the Father of Us All to the cowpoke next door, the early gay literati to rude, queercore mosh rats. No one is better than Bacchus at staking out sexual territory with a swagger and a sly grin.

MASQUERADE BOOKS

BONE
$4.95/177-2
Queer musings from the pen of one of today's hottest young talents. A fresh outlook on fleshly indulgence yields more than a few pleasant surprises. Horny Tom Bacchus maps out the tricking ground of a new generation.

KEY LINCOLN
SUBMISSION HOLDS
$4.95/266-3
A bright young talent unleashes his first collection of gay erotica. From tough to tender, the men between these covers stop at nothing to get what they want. These sweat-soaked tales show just how bad boys can really get.

CALDWELL/EIGHNER
QSFX2
$5.95/278-7
The wickedest, wildest, other-worldliest yarns from two master storytellers—Clay Caldwell and Lars Eighner. Both eroticists take a trip to the furthest reaches of the sexual imagination, sending back ten stories proving that as much as things change, one thing will always remain the same....

CLAY CALDWELL
JOCK STUDS
$6.50/472-0
A collection of Caldwell's scalding tales of pumped bodies and raging libidos. Swimmers, runners, football players... whatever your sport might be, there's a man waiting for you in these pages. Waiting to peel off that uniform and claim his reward for a game well-played....

ASK OL' BUDDY
$5.95/346-5
Set in the underground SM world, Caldwell takes you on a journey of discovery—where men initiate one another into the secrets of the rawest realm of all. And when each stud's initiation is complete, he takes his places among the masters—eager to take part in the training of another hungry soul...

STUD SHORTS
$5.95/320-1
"If anything, Caldwell's charm is more powerful, his nostalgia more poignant, the horniness he captures more sweetly, achingly acute than ever."
—Aaron Travis
A new collection of this legend's latest sex-fiction. With his customary candor, Caldwell tells all about cops, cadets, truckers, farmboys (and many more) in these dirty jewels.

TAILPIPE TRUCKER
$5.95/296-5
Trucker porn! In prose as free and unvarnished as a cross-country highway, Caldwell tells the truth about Trag and Curly—two men hot for the feeling of sweaty mantflesh. Together, they pick up—and turn out—a couple of thrill-seeking punks.

SERVICE, STUD
$5.95/336-8
Another look at the gay future. The setting is the Los Angeles of a distant future. Here the all-male populace is divided between the served and the servants—guaranteeing the erotic satisfaction of all involved.

QUEERS LIKE US
$4.95/262-0
"Caldwell at his most charming." —Aaron Travis
For years the name Clay Caldwell has been synonymous with the hottest, most finely crafted gay tales available. *Queers Like Us* is one of his best: the story of a randy mailman's trek through a landscape of willing, available studs.

ALL-STUD
$4.95/104-7
This classic, sex-soaked tale takes place under the watchful eye of Number Ten: an omniscient figure who has decreed unabashed promiscuity as the law of his all-male land. One stud, however, takes it upon himself to challenge the social order, daring to fall in love. Finally, he is forced to fight for not only himself, but the man he loves.

CLAY CALDWELL AND AARON TRAVIS
TAG TEAM STUDS
$6.50/465-8
Thrilling tales from these two legendary eroticists. The wrestling world will never seem the same, once you've made your way through this assortment of sweaty, virile studs. But you'd better be wary—should one catch you off guard, you just might spend the rest of the night pinned to the mat....

LARRY TOWNSEND
LEATHER AD: S
$5.95/407-0
The second half of Townsend's acclaimed tale of lust through the personals—this time told from a Top's perspective. A simple ad generates many responses, and one man finds himself in the enviable position of putting these studly applicants through their paces....

LEATHER AD: M
$5.95/380-5
The first of this two-part classic. John's curious about what goes on between the leatherclad men he's fantasized about. He takes out a personal ad, and starts a journey of self-discovery that will leave no part of his life unchanged.

---

1 900 745-HUNG

Hardcore phone action for real men. A scorching assembly of studs is waiting for your call—and eager to give you the headtrip of your life! Totally live, guaranteed one-on-one encounters. (Must be over 18.) No credit card needed. $3.98 per minute.

BUY ANY 4 BOOKS & CHOOSE 1 ADDITIONAL BOOK, OF EQUAL OR LESSER VALUE, AS YOUR FREE GIFT

MASQUERADE BOOKS

BEWARE THE GOD WHO SMILES
$5.95/321-X
Two lusty young Americans are transported to ancient Egypt—where they are embroiled in regional warfare and taken as slaves by marauding barbarians. The key to escape from this brutal bondage lies in their own rampant libidos, and urges as old as time itself.

2069 TRILOGY
(This one-volume collection only $6.95)244-2
For the first time, Larry Townsend's early science-fiction trilogy appears in one massive volume! Set in a future world, the *2069 Trilogy* includes the tight plotting and shameless male sexual pleasure that established him as one of gay erotica's first masters.

MIND MASTER
$4.95/209-4
Who better to explore the territory of erotic dominance than an author who helped define the genre—and knows that ultimate mastery always transcends the physical. Another unrelenting Townsend tale.

THE LONG LEATHER CORD
$4.95/201-9
Chuck's stepfather never lacks money or clandestine male visitors with whom he enacts intense sexual rituals. As Chuck comes to terms with his own desires, he begins to unravel the mystery behind his stepfather's secret life.

MAN SWORD
$4.95/188-8
The trés gai tale of France's King Henri III, who was unimaginably spoiled by his mother—the infamous Catherine de Medici—and groomed from a young age to assume the throne of France. Along the way, he encounters enough sexual schemers and politicos to alter one's picture of history forever!

THE FAUSTUS CONTRACT
$4.95/167-5
Two attractive young men desperately need $1000. Will do anything. Travel OK. Danger OK. Call anytime... Two cocky young hustlers get more than they bargained for in this story of lust and its discontents.

THE GAY ADVENTURES OF CAPTAIN GOOSE
$4.95/169-1
Hot young Jerome Gander is sentenced to serve aboard the *H.M.S. Faerigold*—a ship manned by the most hardened, unrepentant criminals. In no time, Gander becomes well-versed in the ways of horny men at sea, and the *Faerigold* becomes the most notorious vessel to ever set sail.

CHAINS
$4.95/158-6
Picking up street punks has always been risky, but in Larry Townsend's classic *Chains*, it sets off a string of events that must be read to be believed.

KISS OF LEATHER
$4.95/161-6
A look at the acts and attitudes of an earlier generation of gay leathermen, Kiss of Leather is full to bursting with the gritty, raw action that has distinguished Townsend's work for years. Sensual pain and pleasure mix in this tightly plotted tale.

RUN, LITTLE LEATHER BOY
$4.95/143-8
One young man's sexual awakening. A chronic underachiever, Wayne seems to be going nowhere fast. He finds himself bored with the everyday—and drawn to the masculine intensity of a dark and mysterious sexual underground, where he soon finds many goals worth pursuing....

RUN NO MORE
$4.95/152-7
The continuation of Larry Townsend's legendary *Run, Little Leather Boy*. This volume follows the further adventures of Townsend's leatherclad narrator as he travels every sexual byway available to the S/M male.

THE SCORPIUS EQUATION
$4.95/119-5
The story of a man caught between the demands of two galactic empires. Our randy hero must match wits—and more—with the incredible forces that rule his world.

THE SEXUAL ADVENTURES OF SHERLOCK HOLMES
$4.95/3097-0
A scandalously sexy take on this legendary sleuth. "A Study in Scarlet" is transformed to expose Mrs. Hudson as a man in drag, the Diogenes Club as an S/M arena, and clues only the redoubtable—and very horny—Sherlock Holmes could piece together. A baffling tale of sex and mystery.

DONALD VINING

CABIN FEVER AND OTHER STORIES
$5.95/338-4
Eighteen blistering stories in celebration of the most intimate of male bonding. Time after time, Donald Vining's men succumb to nature, and reaffirm both love and lust in modern gay life.

"Demonstrates the wisdom experience combined with insight and optimism can create."
—*Bay Area Reporter*

DEREK ADAMS

PRISONER OF DESIRE
$6.50/439-9
Scalding fiction from one of Badboy's most popular authors. The creator of horny P.I. Miles Diamond returns with this volume bursting with red-blooded, sweat-soaked excursions through the modern gay libido.

THE MARK OF THE WOLF
$5.95/361-9
I turned to look at the man who stared back at me from the mirror. The familiar outlines of my face seemed coarser, more sinister. An animal? The past comes back to haunt one well-off stud, whose unslakeable thirsts lead him into the arms of many men—and the midst of a perilous mystery.

MY DOUBLE LIFE
$5.95/314-7
Every man leads a double life, dividing his hours between the mundanities of the day and the outrageous pursuits of the night. The creator of sexy P.I. Miles Diamond shines a little light on the wicked things men do when no one's looking.

MASQUERADE BOOKS

HEAT WAVE
$4.95/159-4
"His body was draped in baggy clothes, but there was hardly any doubt that they covered anything less than perfection.... His slacks were cinched tight around a narrow waist, and the rise of flesh pushing against the thin fabric promised a firm, melon-shaped ass...."

MILES DIAMOND AND THE DEMON OF DEATH
$4.95/251-5
Derek Adams' gay gumshoe returns for further adventures. Miles always finds himself in the stickiest situations—with any stud whose path he crosses! His adventures with "The Demon of Death" promise another carnal carnival.

THE ADVENTURES OF MILES DIAMOND
$4.95/118-7
The debut of Miles Diamond—Derek Adams' take on the classic American archetype of the hardboiled private eye. "The Case of the Missing Twin" promises to be a most rewarding case, packed as it is with randy studs. Miles sets about uncovering all as he tracks down the elusive and delectable Daniel Travis.

KELVIN BELIELE

IF THE SHOE FITS
$4.95/223-X
An essential and winning volume of tales exploring a world where randy boys can't help but do what comes naturally—as often as possible! Sweaty male bodies grapple in pleasure, proving the old adage: if the shoe fits, one might as well slip right in....

JAMES MEDLEY

THE REVOLUTIONARY & OTHER STORIES
$6.50/417-8
Billy, the son of the station chief of the American Embassy in Guatemala, is kidnapped and held for ransom. Frightened at first, Billy gradually develops an unimaginably close relationship with Juan, the revolutionary assigned to guard him.

HUCK AND BILLY
$4.95/245-0
Young love is always the sweetest, always the most sorrowful. Young lust, on the other hand, knows no bounds—and is often the hottest of one's life! Huck and Billy explore the desires that course through their young male bodies, determined to plumb the lusty depths of passion.

FLEDERMAUS

FLEDERFICTION: STORIES OF MEN AND TORTURE
$5.95/355-4
Fifteen blistering paeans to men and their suffering. Fledermaus unleashes his most thrilling tales of punishment in this special volume designed with Badboy readers in mind.

VICTOR TERRY

MASTERS
$6.50/418-6
A powerhouse volume of boot-wearing, whip-wielding, bone-crunching bruisers who've got what it takes to make a grown man grovel. Between these covers lurk the most demanding of men—the imperious few to whom so many humbly offer themselves....

SM/SD
$6.50/406-2
Set around a South Dakota town called Prairie, these tales offer compelling evidence that the real rough stuff can still be found where men roam free of the restraints of "polite" society—and take what they want despite all rules.

WHiPs
$4.95/254-X
Connoisseurs of gay writing have known Victor Terry's work for some time. Cruising for a hot man? You'd better be, because one way or another, these WHiPs—officers of the Wyoming Highway Patrol—are gonna pull you over for a little impromptu interrogation....

MAX EXANDER

DEEDS OF THE NIGHT: TALES OF EROS AND PASSION
$5.95/348-1
MAXimum porn! Exander's a writer who's seen it all—and is more than happy to describe every inch of it in pulsating detail. A whirlwind tour of the hypermasculine libido.

LEATHERSEX
$4.95/210-8
Hard-hitting tales from merciless Max Exander. This time he focuses on the leatherclad lust that draws together only the most willing and talented of tops and bottoms—for an all-out orgy of limitless surrender and control....

MANSEX
$4.95/160-8
"Mark was the classic leatherman: a huge, dark stud in chaps, with a big black moustache, hairy chest and enormous muscles. Exactly the kind of men Todd liked—strong, hunky, masculine, ready to take control...."

TOM CAFFREY

TALES FROM THE MEN'S ROOM
$5.95/364-3
From shameless cops on the beat to shy studs on stage, Caffrey explores male lust at its most elemental and arousing. And if there's a lesson to be learned, it's that the Men's Room is less a place than a state of mind—one that every man finds himself in, day after day....

HITTING HOME
$4.95/222-1
Titillating and compelling, the stories in *Hitting Home* make a strong case for there being only one thing on a man's mind.

BUY ANY 4 BOOKS & CHOOSE 1 ADDITIONAL BOOK, OF EQUAL OR LESSER VALUE, AS YOUR FREE GIFT

MASQUERADE BOOKS

TORSTEN BARRING

GUY TRAYNOR
$6.50/414-3
Some call Guy Traynor a theatrical genius; others say he was a madman. All anyone knows for certain is that his productions were the result of blood, sweat and tears. Never have artists suffered so much for their craft!

PRISONERS OF TORQUEMADA
$5.95/252-3
Another volume sure to push you over the edge. How cruel is the "therapy" practiced at Casa Torquemada? Barring is just the writer to evoke such steamy sexual malevolence.

SHADOWMAN
$4.95/178-0
From spoiled Southern aristocrats to randy youths sowing wild oats at the local picture show, Barring's imagination works overtime in these vignettes of homolust—past, present and future.

PETER THORNWELL
$4.95/149-7
Follow the exploits of Peter Thornwell as he goes from misspent youth to scandalous stardom, all thanks to an insatiable libido and love for the lash.

THE SWITCH
$4.95/3061-X
Sometimes a man needs a good whipping, and *The Switch* certainly makes a case! Packed with hot studs and unrelenting passions.

BERT McKENZIE

FRINGE BENEFITS
$5.95/354-5
From the pen of a widely published short story writer comes a volume of highly immodest tales. Not afraid of getting down and dirty, McKenzie produces some of today's most visceral sextales.

SONNY FORD

REUNION IN FLORENCE
$4.95/3070-9
Captured by Turks, Adrian and Tristan will do anything to save their heads. When Tristan is threatened by a Sultan's jealousy, Adrian begins his quest for the only man alive who can replace Tristan as the object of the Sultan's lust.

ROGER HARMAN

FIRST PERSON
$4.95/179-9
A highly personal collection. Each story takes the form of a confessional—told by men who've got plenty to confess! From the "first time ever" to firsts of different kinds, *First Person* tells truths too hot to be purely fiction.

J. A. GUERRA, ED.

SLOW BURN
$4.95/3042-3
Welcome to the Body Shoppe! Torsos get lean and hard, pecs widen, and stomachs ripple in these sexy stories of the power and perils of physical perfection.

DAVE KINNICK

SORRY I ASKED
$4.95/3090-3
Unexpurgated interviews with gay porn's rank and file. Get personal with the men behind (and under) the "stars," and discover the hot truth about the porn business.

SEAN MARTIN

SCRAPBOOK
$4.95/224-8
Imagine a book filled with only the best, most vivid remembrances...a book brimming with every hot, sexy encounter its pages can hold... Now you need only open up *Scrapbook* to know that such a volume really exists....

CARO SOLES & STAN TAL, EDITORS

BIZARRE DREAMS
$4.95/187-X
An anthology of stirring voices dedicated to exploring the dark side of human fantasy. *Bizarre Dreams* brings together the most talented practitioners of "dark fantasy," the most forbidden sexual realm of all.

CHRISTOPHER MORGAN

STEAM GAUGE
$6.50/473-9
This volume abounds in manly men doing what they do best—to, with, or for any hot stud who crosses their paths. Frequently published to acclaim in the gay press, Christopher Morgan puts a fresh, contemporary spin on the very oldest of urges.

THE SPORTSMEN
$5.95/385-6
A collection of super-hot stories dedicated to that most popular of boys next door—the all-American athlete. Here are enough tales of carnal gram slams, sexy interceptions and highly personal bests to satisfy the hungers of the most ardent sports fan. Editor Christopher Morgan has gathered those writers who know just the type of guys that make up every red-blooded male's starting line-up....

MUSCLE BOUND
$4.95/3028-8
In the New York City bodybuilding scene, country boy Tommy joins forces with sexy Will Rodriguez in a battle of wits and biceps at the hottest gym in town, where the weak are bound and crushed by iron-pumping gods.

MICHAEL LOWENTHAL, ED.

THE BADBOY EROTIC LIBRARY VOLUME I
$4.95/190-X
Excerpts from *A Secret Life*, *Imre*, *Sins of the Cities of the Plain*, *Teleny* and others demonstrate the uncanny gift for portraying sex between men that led to many of these titles being banned upon publication.

THE BADBOY EROTIC LIBRARY VOLUME II
$4.95/211-6
This time, selections are taken from *Mike and Me* and *Muscle Bound*, *Men at Work*, *Badboy Fantasies*, and *Slowburn*.

MASQUERADE BOOKS

ERIC BOYD

MIKE AND ME
$5.95/419-4
Mike joined the gym squad to bulk up on muscle. Little did he know he'd be turning on every sexy muscle jock in Minnesota! Hard bodies collide in a series of workouts designed to generate a whole lot more than rips and cuts.

MIKE AND THE MARINES
$6.50/497-6
Mike takes on America's most elite corps of studs—running into more than a few good men! Join in on the never-ending sexual escapades of this singularly lustful platoon!

ANONYMOUS

A SECRET LIFE
$4.95/3017-2
Meet Master Charles: only eighteen, and quite innocent, until his arrival at the Sir Percival's Royal Academy, where the daily lessons are supplemented with a crash course in pure, sweet sexual heat!

SINS OF THE CITIES OF THE PLAIN
$5.95/322-8
Indulge yourself in the scorching memoirs of young man-about-town Jack Saul. With his shocking dalliances with the lords and "ladies" of British high society, Jack's positively sinful escapades grow wilder with every chapter!

IMRE
$4.95/3019-9
What dark secrets, what fiery passions lay hidden behind strikingly beautiful Lieutenant Imre's emerald eyes? An extraordinary lost classic of fantasy, obsession, gay erotic desire, and romance in a small European town on the eve of WWI.

TELENY
$4.95/3020-2
Often attributed to Oscar Wilde, *Teleny* tells the story of one young man of independent means. He dedicates himself to a succession of forbidden pleasures, but instead finds love and tragedy when he becomes embroiled in a cult devoted to fulfilling only the very darkest of fantasies.

HARD CANDY

KEVIN KILLIAN

ARCTIC SUMMER
$6.95/514-X
Highly acclaimed author Kevin Killian's latest novel examines the many secrets lying beneath the placid exterior of America in the '50s. With the story of Liam Reilly—a young gay man of considerable means and numerous secrets—Killian exposes the contradictions of the American Dream, and the ramifications of the choices one is forced to make when hiding the truth.

STAN LEVENTHAL

BARBIE IN BONDAGE
$6.95/415-1
Widely regarded as one of the most refreshing, clear-eyed interpreters of big city gay male life, Leventhal here provides a series of explorations of love and desire between men. Uncompromising, but gentle and generous, *Barbie in Bondage* is a fitting tribute to the late author's unique talents.

SKYDIVING ON CHRISTOPHER STREET
$6.95/287-6
"Positively addictive." —Dennis Cooper
Aside from a hateful job, a hateful apartment, a hateful world and an increasingly hateful lover, life seems, well, all right for the protagonist of Stan Leventhal's latest novel. Having already lost most of his friends to AIDS, how could things get any worse? But things soon do, and he's forced to endure much more....

PATRICK MOORE

IOWA
$6.95/423-2
"Moore is the Tennessee Williams of the nineties—profound intimacy freed in a compelling narrative."
—Karen Finley
"Fresh and shiny and relevant to our time. *Iowa* is full of terrific characters etched in acid-sharp prose, soaked through with just enough ambivalence to make it thoroughly romantic." —Felice Picano
A stunning novel about one gay man's journey into adulthood, and the roads that bring him home again.

PAUL T. ROGERS

SAUL'S BOOK
$7.95/462-3
Winner of the Editors' Book Award
"Exudes an almost narcotic power.... A masterpiece." —*Village Voice Literary Supplement*
"A first novel of considerable power... Sinbad the Sailor, thanks to the sympathetic imagination of Paul T. Rogers, speaks to us all." —*New York Times Book Review*
The story of a Times Square hustler called Sinbad the Sailor and Saul, a brilliant, self-destructive, alcoholic, thoroughly dominating character who may be the only love Sinbad will ever know.

WALTER R. HOLLAND

THE MARCH
$6.95/429-1
A moving testament to the power of friendship during even the worst of times. Beginning on a hot summer night in 1980, *The March* revolves around a circle of young gay men, and the many others their lives touch. Over time, each character changes in unexpected ways; lives and loves come together and fall apart, as society itself is horribly altered by the onslaught of AIDS.

BUY ANY 4 BOOKS & CHOOSE 1 ADDITIONAL BOOK, OF EQUAL OR LESSER VALUE, AS YOUR FREE GIFT

MASQUERADE BOOKS

RED JORDAN AROBATEAU
LUCY AND MICKEY
$6.95/311-2
The story of Mickey—an uncompromising butch—and her long affair with Lucy, the femme she loves. A raw tale of pre-Stonewall lesbian life.
"A necessary reminder to all who blissfully—some may say ignorantly—ride the wave of lesbian chic into the mainstream." —Heather Findlay

DIRTY PICTURES
$5.95/345-7
"Red Jordan Arobateau is the Thomas Wolfe of lesbian literature... She's a natural—raw talent that is seething, passionate, hard, remarkable."
—Lillian Faderman, editor of *Chloe Plus Olivia*
Dirty Pictures is the story of a lonely butch tending bar—and the femme she finally calls her own.

DONALD VINING
A GAY DIARY
$8.95/451-8
Donald Vining's *Diary* portrays a long-vanished age and the lifestyle of a gay generation all too frequently forgotten.
"*A Gay Diary* is, unquestionably, the richest historical document of gay male life in the United States that I have ever encountered.... It illuminates a critical period in gay male American history."
—*Body Politic*

LARS EIGHNER
GAY COSMOS
$6.95/236-1
A title sure to appeal not only to Eighner's gay fans, but the many converts who first encountered his moving nonfiction work. Praised by the press, *Gay Cosmos* is an important contribution to the area of Gay and Lesbian Studies.

FELICE PICANO
THE LURE
$6.95/398-8
"The subject matter, plus the authenticity of Picano's research are, combined, explosive. Felice Picano is one hell of a writer." —Stephen King
After witnessing a brutal murder, Noel is recruited by the police, to assist as a lure for the killer. Undercover, he moves deep into the freneticism of Manhattan's gay highlife—where he gradually becomes aware of the darker forces at work in his life. In addition to the mystery behind his mission, he begins to recognize changes: in his relationships with the men around him, in himself...

AMBIDEXTROUS
$6.95/275-2
"Makes us remember what it feels like to be a child..."
—*The Advocate*
Picano's first "memoir in the form of a novel" tells all: home life, school face-offs, the ingenuous sophistications of his first sexual steps. In three years' time, he's had his first gay fling—and is on his way to becoming the widely praised writer he is today.

MEN WHO LOVED ME
$6.95/274-4
"Zesty...spiked with adventure and romance...a distinguished and humorous portrait of a vanished age." —*Publishers Weekly*
In 1966, Picano abandoned New York, determined to find true love in Europe. Upon returning, he plunges into the city's thriving gay community of the 1970s.

WILLIAM TALSMAN
THE GAUDY IMAGE
$6.95/263-9
"To read *The Gaudy Image* now...it is to see firsthand the very issues of identity and positionality with which gay men were struggling in the decades before Stonewall. For what Talsman is dealing with...is the very question of how we conceive ourselves gay."
—from the introduction by Michael Bronski

ROSEBUD

THE ROSEBUD READER
$5.95/319-8
Rosebud has contributed greatly to the burgeoning genre of lesbian erotica—to the point that our authors are among the hottest and most closely watched names in lesbian and gay publishing. Here are the finest moments from Rosebud's contemporary classics.

LESLIE CAMERON
WHISPER OF FANS
$6.50/542-5
"Just looking into her eyes, she felt that she knew a lot about this woman. She could see strength, boldness, a fresh sense of aliveness that rocked her to the core. In turn she felt open, revealed under the woman's gaze—all her secrets already told. No need of shame or artifice...." A fresh tale of passion between women, from one of lesbian erotica's up-and-coming authors.

RACHEL PEREZ
ODD WOMEN
$6.50/526-3
These women are sexy, smart, tough—some even say odd. But who cares, when their combined ass-ets are so sweet! An assortment of Sapphic sirens proves once and for all that comely ladies come best in pairs.

RANDY TUROFF
LUST NEVER SLEEPS
$6.50/475-5
A rich volume of highly erotic, powerfully real fiction from the editor of *Lesbian Words*. Randy Turoff depicts a circle of modern women connected through the bonds of love, friendship, ambition, and lust with accuracy and compassion. Moving, tough, yet undeniably true, Turoff's stories create a stirring portrait of contemporary lesbian life and community.

MASQUERADE BOOKS

RED JORDAN AROBATEAU

ROUGH TRADE
$6.50/470-4
Famous for her unflinching portrayal of lower-class dyke life and love, Arobateau outdoes herself with these tales of butch/femme affairs and unrelenting passions. Unapologetic and distinctly non-homogenized, *Rough Trade* is a must for all fans of challenging lesbian literature.

BOYS NIGHT OUT
$6.50/463-1
A *Red*-hot volume of short fiction from this lesbian literary sensation. As always, Arobateau takes a good hard look at the lives of everyday women, noting well the struggles and triumphs each woman experiences.

ALISON TYLER

VENUS ONLINE
$6.50/521-2
What's my idea of paradise? Lovely Alexa spends her days in a boring bank job, not quite living up to her full potential—interested instead in saving her energies for her nocturnal pursuits. At night, Alexa goes online, living out virtual adventures that become more real with each session. Soon Alexa—aka Venus—feels her erotic imagination growing beyond anything she could have imagined.

DARK ROOM: AN ONLINE ADVENTURE
$6.50/455-0
Dani, a successful photographer, can't bring herself to face the death of her lover, Kate. An ambitious journalist, Kate was found mysteriously murdered, leaving her lover with only fond memories of a too-brief relationship. Determined to keep the memory of her lover alive, Dani goes online under Kate's screen alias—and begins to uncover the truth behind the crime that has torn her world apart.

BLUE SKY SIDEWAYS & OTHER STORIES
$6.50/394-5
A variety of women, and their many breathtaking experiences with lovers, friends—and even the occasional sexy stranger. From blossoming young beauties to fearless vixens, Tyler finds the sexy pleasures of everyday life.

DIAL "L" FOR LOVELESS
$5.95/386-4
Meet Katrina Loveless—a private eye talented enough to give Sam Spade a run for his money. In her first case, Katrina investigates a murder implicating a host of society's darlings. Loveless untangles the mess—while working herself into a variety of highly compromising knots with the many lovelies who cross her path!

THE VIRGIN
$5.95/379-1
Veronica answers a personal ad in the "Women Seeking Women" category—and discovers a whole sensual world she never knew existed! And she never dreamed she'd be prized as a virgin all over again, by someone who would deflower her with a passion no man could ever show....

K. T. BUTLER

TOOLS OF THE TRADE
$5.95/420-8
A sparkling mix of lesbian erotica and humor. An encounter with ice cream, cappuccino and chocolate cake; an affair with a complete stranger; a pair of faulty handcuffs; and love on a drafting table. Seventeen tales.

LOVECHILD

GAG
$5.95/369-4
From New York's poetry scene comes this explosive volume of work from one of the bravest, most cutting young writers you'll ever encounter. The poems in *Gag* take on American hypocrisy with uncommon energy, and announce Lovechild as a writer of unforgettable rage.

ELIZABETH OLIVER

PAGAN DREAMS
$5.95/295-7
Cassidy and Samantha plan a vacation at a secluded bed-and-breakfast, hoping for a little personal time alone. Their hostess, however, has different plans. The lovers are plunged into a world of dungeons and pagan rites, as Anastasia steals Samantha for her own.

SUSAN ANDERS

CITY OF WOMEN
$5.95/375-9
Stories dedicated to women and the passions that draw them together. Designed strictly for the sensual pleasure of women, these tales are set to ignite flames of passion from coast to coast.

PINK CHAMPAGNE
$5.95/282-5
Tasty, torrid tales of butch/femme couplings. Tough as nails or soft as silk, these women seek out their antitheses, intent on working out the details of their own personal theory of difference.

ANONYMOUS

LAVENDER ROSE
$4.95/208-6
From the writings of Sappho, Queen of the island Lesbos, to the turn-of-the-century *Black Book of Lesbianism*; from *Tips to Maidens* to *Crimson Hairs*, a recent lesbian saga—here are the great but little-known lesbian writings and revelations.

LAURA ANTONIOU, EDITOR

LEATHERWOMEN
$4.95/3095-4
These fantasies, from the pens of new or emerging authors, break every rule imposed on women's fantasies. The hottest stories from some of today's newest and most outrageous writers make this an unforgettable exploration of the female libido.

BUY ANY 4 BOOKS & CHOOSE 1 ADDITIONAL BOOK, OF EQUAL OR LESSER VALUE, AS YOUR FREE GIFT

MASQUERADE BOOKS

LEATHERWOMEN II
$4.95/229-9
Another groundbreaking volume of writing from women on the edge, sure to ignite libidinal flames in any reader. Leave taboos behind, because these Leatherwomen know no limits....

AARONA GRIFFIN
PASSAGE AND OTHER STORIES
$4.95/3057-1
An S/M romance. Lovely Nina is frightened by her lesbian passions, until she finds herself infatuated with a woman she spots at a local café. One night Nina follows her, and finds herself enmeshed in an endless maze leading to a world where women test the edges of sexuality and power.

VALENTINA CILESCU
MY LADY'S PLEASURE: MISTRESS WITH A MAID, VOLUME I
$5.95/412-7
Claudia Dungarrow, a lovely, powerful, but mysterious professor, attempts to seduce virginal Elizabeth Stanbridge, setting off a chain of events that eventually ruins her career. Claudia vows revenge—and makes her foes pay deliciously....

DARK VENUS: MISTRESS WITH A MAID, VOLUME 2
$6.50/481-X
This thrilling saga of cruel lust continues! *Mistress with a Maid* breathes new life into the conventions of dominance and submission. What emerges is a picture of unremitting desire—whether it be for supreme erotic power or ultimate sexual surrender.

BODY AND SOUL: MISTRESS WITH A MAID 3
$6.50/515-8
The blistering conclusion to lesbian erotica's most unsparing trilogy! Dr. Claudia Dungarrow returns for yet another tour of depravity, subjugating every maiden in sight to her ruthless sexual whims. But, as stunning as Claudia is, she has yet to hold Elizabeth Stanbridge in complete submission. Will she ever?

THE ROSEBUD SUTRA
$4.95/242-6
"Women are hardly ever known in their true light, though they may love others, or become indifferent towards them, may give them delight, or abandon them, or may extract from them all the wealth that they possess." So says *The Rosebud Sutra*—a volume promising women's inner secrets.

MISTRESS MINE
$6.50/502-6
Sophia Cranleigh sits in prison, accused of authoring the "obscene" *Mistress Mine*. What she has done, however, is merely chronicle the events of her life. For Sophia has led no ordinary life, but has slaved and suffered—deliciously—under the hand of the notorious Mistress Malin. The uncensored tale of a life of sensuous suffering, by one of today's hottest lesbian writers.

LINDSAY WELSH
SECOND SIGHT
$6.50/507-7
The debut of Dana Steele—lesbian superhero! During an attack by a gang of homophobic youths, Dana is thrown onto subway tracks—touching the deadly third rail. Miraculously, she survives, and finds herself endowed with superhuman powers. Dana decides to devote her powers to the protection of her lesbian sisters, no matter how daunting the danger they face.

NASTY PERSUASIONS
$6.50/436-4
A hot peek into the behind-the-scenes operations of Rough Trade—one of the world's most famous lesbian clubs. Join Slash, Ramone, Cherry and many others as they bring one another to the height of torturous ecstasy—all in the name of keeping Rough Trade the premier name in sexy entertainment for women.

MILITARY SECRETS
$5.95/397-X
Colonel Candice Sproule heads a highly specialized boot camp. Assisted by three dominatrix sergeants, Col. Sproule takes on the talented submissives sent to her by secret military contacts. Then along comes Jesse—whose pleasure in being served matches the Colonel's own. This horny new recruit sets off fireworks in the barracks—and beyond....

ROMANTIC ENCOUNTERS
$5.95/359-7
Beautiful Julie, the most powerful editor of romance novels in the industry, spends her days igniting women's passions through books—and her nights fulfilling those needs with a variety of licentious lovers. Finally, through a sizzling series of coincidences, Julie's two worlds come together explosively!

THE BEST OF LINDSAY WELSH
$5.95/368-6
A collection of this popular writer's best work. Lindsay Welsh was one of Rosebud's early bestsellers, and remains one of our most popular writers. This sampler is set to introduce some of the hottest lesbian erotica to a wider audience.

NECESSARY EVIL
$5.95/277-9
What's a girl to do? When her Mistress proves too systematic, too by-the-book, one lovely submissive takes the ultimate chance—choosing and creating a Mistress who'll fulfill her heart's desire. Little did she know how difficult it would be—and, in the end, rewarding....

A VICTORIAN ROMANCE
$5.95/365-1
Lust-letters from the road. A young Englishwoman realizes her dream—a trip abroad under the guidance of her eccentric maiden aunt. Soon, the young but blossoming Elaine comes to discover her own sexual talents, as a hot-blooded Parisian named Madelaine takes her Sapphic education in hand.

ORDERING IS EASY

MC/VISA orders can be placed by calling our toll-free number
PHONE 800-375-2356/FAX 212-986-7355/E-MAIL masqbks@aol.com
or mail this coupon to:
MASQUERADE DIRECT
DEPT. BMBB17 801 2ND AVE., NY, NY 10017

BUY ANY FOUR BOOKS AND CHOOSE ONE ADDITIONAL BOOK, OF EQUAL OR LESSER VALUE, AS YOUR FREE GIFT.

QTY.	TITLE	NO.	PRICE
			FREE
			FREE

We Never Sell, Give or Trade Any Customer's Name.

SUBTOTAL
POSTAGE and HANDLING
TOTAL

In the U.S., please add $1.50 for the first book and 75¢ for each additional book; in Canada, add $2.00 for the first book and $1.25 for each additional book. Foreign countries: add $4.00 for the first book and $2.00 for each additional book. No C.O.D. orders. Please make all checks payable to Masquerade Books. Payable in U.S. currency only. New York state residents add 8.25% sales tax. Please allow 4-6 weeks for delivery.

NAME _____

ADDRESS _____

CITY _____ STATE _____ ZIP _____

TEL( ) _____

E-MAIL _____

PAYMENT: ☐ CHECK   ☐ MONEY ORDER   ☐ VISA   ☐ MC

CARD NO _____ EXP. DATE _____